Withdrawn

W9-BVT-331

ILLINOIS CENTRAL COLLEGE
DS557.A6G6
STACKS
Triumph or tragedy;

A12900 407137

DS
557   GOOL
.A6   Triumph or tragedy
G6

Illinois Central College
Learning Resource Center

Books by Richard N. Goodwin

The Sowers Seed

Triumph or Tragedy
Reflections on Vietnam

Triumph or Tragedy

Reflections on Vietnam

Triumph or Tragedy

Reflections on Vietnam

RICHARD N. GOODWIN

RANDOM HOUSE

New York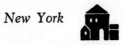

ILLINOIS CENTRAL COLLEGE
LEARNING RESOURCE CENTER

35831

DS
557
.A6
E6

First Printing

© Copyright, 1966, by Richard N. Goodwin

All rights reserved under International and
Pan American Copyright Conventions.
Published in New York by Random House, Inc.
Distributed in Toronto, Canada,
by Random House of Canada Limited.

Map on page 143 courtesy of *The New York Times.*
© 1966 by The New York Times Company.
Reprinted by permission.

Library of Congress Catalog Card Number: 66-23612

Manufactured in the United States of America
by the Colonial Press Inc., Clinton, Mass.

Except for the Postscript and the Appendix,
the contents of this book appeared originally
as an article in *The New Yorker.*

To Paul Horgan and the
Centre for Advanced Studies at
Wesleyan University

Contents

Triumph or Tragedy

Reflections on Vietnam

It must have seemed to the commander who made the choice that Operation White Wing had a faintly lyrical sound, suited to the An Lao Valley, where battle was to be found and fought. Dark-green jungle flows over gentle hills toward flat, still swamps, bursting with rice and separated by the trailing wisps of jungle growth that spring up wherever the hand of man pauses to rest. The river slices south through the center of the valley until, north of Bong Son, it turns east toward the South China Sea. The river was muddy —as it always is at the end of January, when the rains are heavy—perhaps reminding Pfcs. James Ricks and Harry Morse of the upper waters of the Potomac, which divides their native states of Maryland and Virginia. It was about as wide, and there were rapids. But there was nothing at home like the soaking heat that crowded their lungs, or the violent nighttime fury that tore about the bunker where they waited for dawn. The two friends had come with the 18th Infantry to help clear An Lao of the thousands of Vietcong guerrillas who made their home in the bountiful valley.

Eleven thousand miles away, where the Potomac broadens, senators and spectators walked into Room 4221 of the New Senate Office Building. J. William Fulbright, Senator from Arkansas, foe of civil rights, almost Secretary of State, Rhodes Scholar and backwoods politician, hero to some and demagogue to others, sat in the center chair behind the raised, arched desk that stretched across the entire front of the rectangular hearing room. The marble margins of the floor touched light wood-panelled walls in an unsuccessful blending of political-traditional and Washington-modern. In front of Senator Fulbright were officials and clerks bent over tables piled with papers and documents —the vital substance of government—while about sixty spectators filled rows of harsh straight chairs behind them. On either side of Fulbright were the other members of the Senate Committee on Foreign Relations. Among them was Senator Bourke Hickenlooper, of Iowa, tough, narrow, conservative, and, on this day, guardian of the political interests of the Republican Party. Senators Frank Church, of Idaho, and Claiborne Pell, of Rhode Island, were clearly marked, in youth and intelligence, as members of the Kennedy generation of Democrats. There was Stuart Symington, of Missouri, disappointed Presidential hopeful, blending absolute integrity with lifelong sympathy for the aims and outlook of the military. Finally, most vocal in opposition was Wayne Morse, cattle breeder, Oregon Republican-turned-Democrat, who had broken all the rules of the "club" and transgressed the tenets of polite political discourse, thus earning the disdain of official Washington, yet still commanding deference as chairman of a powerful Senate subcommittee, and whose stern, shrill, sometimes exasperatingly self-righteous independence had carried further across the country than Washington believed. Most of the nineteen members were there. The subject was that confused and violent conflict which in the last year had become the center of American concern, expectation, and fear—the war in Vietnam.

Over the chairman's head was the Great Seal of the United States, the eagle gripping the olive branch of peace and the arrows of war—a sculptured omen of the day. Facing him, in a large red-padded chair, sat the first witness—Dean Rusk, for five years Secretary of State of the United States, selected after President-elect Kennedy had reluctantly turned away from Fulbright himself, and the principal advocate of a militant pursuit of the war.

At 9:05 A.M. of Friday, January 28th, the Vietnam debate began. Its subject: the history, the wisdom, and the future of American action and policy. Whatever the result, however discussion might alter the course of events, it would not make any difference to James Ricks, of Cortland, Virginia, or Harry Morse, of Pasadena, Maryland. Twenty minutes before, while the first curious arrivals were claiming the scarce seats, a grenade flung anonymously through the jungle-fed night had exploded in their bunker. They were dead— two more of the almost four hundred thousand people, yellow, white, and black, who had been killed in the strangest and most complicated war in American history.

Before the month of debate was over, it had moved from the small hearing room into the television-dominated homes of millions of Americans, had caused one of the most respected executives in television, Fred Friendly, to quit in fury because his superiors at C.B.S. refused to show the most important national discussion of all, and had made national celebrities out of a soft-spoken general-turned-businessman named James Gavin and a career-diplomat-turned-scholar named George Kennan. With the echoes of the final Friday hearing still fading, the debate touched the upper reaches of American politics. On the morning of Saturday, February 19th, Senator Robert Kennedy discussed the possible outlines of a settlement. He was supported by General Maxwell Taylor, Presidential consultant on the war and intellectual leader of the generals, while he was attacked by other officials, some of whom had privately urged the same position they now publicly assaulted. For a moment, a major political skirmish seemed possible, but the President himself refused to attack the Kennedy proposal. He was clearly determined to close no door that might lead to peace and to open no wounds that might further increase domestic division. Then, the debate having run its course in Washington, it moved into the outer arena of national discussion and the inner secret councils of the administration, where it will continue as long as the war itself.

There is something oddly insubstantial about the thousands of pages of hearings, speeches, press conferences, and television interviews—the immense stream of argument, discussion, and declamation. The pages are filled with rhetoric designed to arouse old emotions rather than stir new thoughts; with grand simplicities and sweeping clichés that ignore and blanket the cruel particulars of conflict; and with history that is neither relevant nor, in many cases, true. Men become advocates rather than analysts, seeking to prove every point and answer every argument, even though they must distort or accuse in order to do so. Some must rewrite the events of the past in order to offer a better defense of their own past acts and judgments. Meanwhile, sensed by all but the scholars is the silent and unseen weight of the American electorate, whose ultimate judgment has never been so unclear in any other time of war, and whose decision will shape the personal futures of those who contest before the gaze of the nation. Each one who speaks is also aware that he speaks across the city to the single man who has the power to gather up all the threads of possibility and belief and weave them into the fabric of decision. Senator Albert Gore said of the President, "We are seeking to reach him by way of the people." Yet each also hoped to reach him by way of the television screen or the morning newspaper.

Much of Vietnam is covered with what experts call "three-canopied jungle." Three layers of sombre, unrelieved green block the sun from the earth, which even at noon is often night-dark. The debate that swirls about this jungle country is also triple-layered, and the tangled lines of argument often obscure the light.

Rising above the other debates is the debate over grand strategy, conducted in the fascinating, elusive abstractions of geopolitics: Does America have a vital stake in Asia, and, more specifically, in Vietnam itself?

Next is the debate over the past: What kind of war is it, and how did we become so deeply involved in it?

Closest to the ground of action and decision is the third Vietnam debate: What is our present policy, and what should it be?

In its crudest and simplest form, the first of the three clashes of conviction questions whether the United States would be seriously injured if much of Asia were to be dominated by a hostile power— at this moment in history, by China. For at least a quarter of a century, every American government has believed the answer to be yes. On November 26, 1941, Secretary of State Cordell Hull handed a series of proposed agreements to the Japanese Ambassador in Washington. Japan and the United States would agree that neither would violate "the territorial integrity and sovereignty" of any country in Asia. Both nations would pledge to seek a broad agreement by many powers, including Great Britain, China, and the Netherlands, "to respect the territorial integrity of French Indo-China [including Vietnam]," and, if that integrity was menaced, to consult "with a view to taking such measures as may be deemed necessary and advisable to meet such threat." (A similar agreement, by many of the same powers, was to become the central guarantee of the Southeast Asia Collective Defense

9

Treaty fourteen years later.) Japan, however, had already determined upon the conquest of Indo-China, and, eleven days later, attacked the only remaining power both committed and able to bar the way. Since the end of the war that followed, every American President has sent armed force to Asia: Truman in Korea, Eisenhower at Quemoy and Matsu, Kennedy briefly at the Thai-Laotian border and in Vietnam, Johnson in Vietnam. Deeply rooted in modern experience, asserted in two major wars, the Amercan interest in Asia, and now in Indo-China, nevertheless requires evaluation by the light of shifting realities. Although the American stake in Asia is not a new one, is it real?

During several years I spent in Washington—at the State Department and as an assistant to Presidents Kennedy and Johnson—few intellectual tasks were more frustrating than the occasional effort to answer the great, the ultimate questions of foreign policy: Why should we try to contain China? Why should we help the underdeveloped nations? What is the urgency of preventing nuclear spread? Such questions, in fact, are ordinarily raised in argument with critics but rarely in the councils of decision. It is precisely because there is no sure and resistless logic by which such questions can be answered that discussion often dissolves into empty generalities and false scholarship. "Nations must learn to leave their neighbors alone." (Cf. the intervention in the Dominican Republic.) We cannot remain "an oasis of wealth in a worldwide sea of misery." (We have always been one and will be one for a very long time.) "The appetite of aggression is never satisfied." (Cf. the independence of the Philippines, Mexico, and Canada.) Such failures of analysis reflect not our own inadequacies so much as what Arthur Schlesinger, Jr., calls "the inscrutability of history." To justify a course of policy in its largest dimension is to predict what will happen if that course is not taken, to prophesy the unknowable turns of history. All that any leader can do is call upon wisdom, judgment, and national principle, a sense of history and a knowledge of present reality, and act on the speculative and intuitive guess that results. This enormous limitation is reflected in Albert Einstein's famous reply when he was asked why the politicians could not catch up with the creations of science—he said that "politics is much harder than physics"—and in George Kennan's testimony that "the most important thing a government such as ours can have, as it faces the long-term future of international relations, is right principles rather than the gift of prophecy." The huge and inescapable uncertainties of this process impose on any sensible statesman an essential skepticism, from which flow at least two guiding rules for the conduct of international affairs: to decide as little, in places of danger, as present urgencies require, leaving room for change if events contradict judgment, and to take as few risks as action requires, refusing to hazard enormous consequences on speculation. The most frequent flaw in the Vietnam debate, running through the arguments on all sides, is the recurrent claim that the unknowable can be stated with certainty.

Even with this caution, judgment leans heavily toward protecting Asia from dominion or conquest by a hostile power. There is the almost idealistic, compelling conviction that the one nation with the power to prevent it should not stand aside while nations unwillingly submit to foreign domination. To do so would undermine the central world purpose of the United States—the creation of an international order of independent states. Moreover, the impact of a large-scale Chinese expansion would probably radiate across the world, reshaping the politics of the weak and uncertain societies of Africa and Latin America, perhaps further eroding the ties among our Western allies, forcing the Soviet Union toward increased militance in the competition for leadership of the Communist world. More ominous still would be the likely effect on our own society. As the fall of China itself contributed to McCarthyism, a large expansion of

China, soon to hold major North American cities hostage to its nuclear power, thus increasing its willingness to risk conflict on the ground, would inevitably feed the dark undercurrent of repression and militarism never wholly absent from American life.

Our vital concern in Asia cannot be denied by allocating that continent to the abstraction of a Chinese "sphere of influence," if by influence we mean domination or the right to direct policies by coercion. Geography is still important, as the Soviet Union learned in Cuba, and as we rediscovered in Hungary. Yet we are as close to Asia, in terms of swift and effective action, as we were to Europe in the Second World War. We are a Pacific nation, and since the end of the Second World War we have been the only Pacific power of real consequence. Moreover, nations have no natural or God-given right to dominate those close to them. If they had, the border states of Afghanistan and Iran would be under Soviet rule; Cuba would be in the hands of a friendly president or, more likely, an American-trained general; Argentina would never have dared admire and assist the Nazis. The sphere of influence of a great nation extends just as far as its power and ambition go unchecked by its own limitations and by the strength and the interests of others. Its "sphere of influence," as domination, rests on the weakness of those in its path, not on the laws of geography or history. China must always weigh heavily in the calculations of Asian states, but as long as our power stands in the way, there need be no vast and inevitable sphere of influence, although it is hoped that there will one day be fruitful relations of commerce and friendship. Nor can we stand aside in the certainty that, as in Eastern Europe, the spread of Communist influence will be blunted by "polycentrism"—a host of Titos, or even Gomulkas. The underdeveloped societies of Asia lack the structures—the middle class, an educated population, even national traditions—that lend strength to the self-assertions of the countries of Europe. The Asian societies are thin at the top, unstable, and far more vulnerable to control by small, well-organized groups assisted from other countries. Nationalist Communism may come to Asia, but the experience of Eastern Europe is no guarantee. We do not know whether China will try to expand, or whether it can. It is hard enough to judge the intentions, ambitions, and capacities of our own leaders. How can we hope to penetrate the thoughts of aging leaders whose experience, culture, and convictions are so remote? This does not mean, however, that we should not be prepared to resist expansion if it comes. Yet, even if we accept this basic judgment, we are not compelled to fight for every inch of Asian soil or hazard war each time Chinese influence begins to grow. We stood by while China crushed Tibet, for we lacked both the resources and any compelling reasons to oppose Chinese armies in such a remote and difficult place. Our government was fully resigned to the potential domination of Indonesia by a Communist Party close to Peking, since armed invasion seemed the only way to prevent it. Nor are American armies likely to rush to the defense of Siberia if Chinese forces move into that vast and tempting area. It is, on the other hand, inconceivable that aggression against India would not be met with—if necessary—the full force of American power. The question always is where, and under what circumstances, we should commit military force to the protection of Asian nations. Is Vietnam such a place?

Not very many years ago, the answer seemed clear. South Vietnam, a tiny patch of poverty-stricken jungle, populated mostly by simple farmers concerned only with the daily struggle for survival, was not important to our security. President Eisenhower, despite urgent French pleas, refused to intervene in 1954 even if all of Vietnam should fall, declaring himself to be "convinced that the French could not win the war." Had the Communists succeeded in taking over the entire country, as they almost did, no sensible American would now be demanding that we go to war to recapture South Vietnam. It would be another name on the list of half-forgotten lost lands. Today, however, events have overtaken that possibility. American power and wealth are committed to Vietnam on an immense scale. We will soon, in all probability, have half a million men in South Vietnam. Helicopters, air support, and modern firearms give our troops there four or five times the striking power of their Second World War counterparts. We have already dropped the rough equivalent of a ton of bombs for every Vietcong soldier. Our financial assistance since 1954 amounts to over three billion dollars, or more than two hundred dollars for every person in South Vietnam. The records are filled with dozens of statements asserting our determination to use force to halt armed aggression. For the United States, after so overwhelming a commitment, to permit a rapid Communist takeover by withdrawal, or, in the President's words, "under the cloak of a meaningless agreement," would damage the confidence of all Asian nations, and of many other nations, in the willingness and the ability of the United States to protect them against attack. Unpleasant and undesirable as it may be for Americans and Asians both, we are the only power strong enough to offer such protection. On the very day that India and China clashed on their border, representatives of India were in Washington to seek assurances of help. They had nowhere else to go. Had we chosen not to intervene in Vietnam, the credibility of our military power would perhaps not be at stake. But those decisions were made. Prince Sihanouk of Cambodia foresaw the way in which increasing American intervention would raise the stakes, telling an interviewer in July, 1965, "It is certain that if the United States provokes a major confrontation in this region—which will inevitably end in [its] humiliating retreat—all the other Asian nations, one after another (beginning with the Allies of the United States), will come to know, if not domination, at least a very strong Communist influence." The battle, therefore, has come to transcend the issue of Vietnam itself, making withdrawal intolerable until we achieve a resolution that does not involve American defeat.

Since there exists such a compelling case, resting, as Dean Rusk testified, "upon policy and strategic and geopolitical considerations that are of the utmost importance," it is baffling to find many supporters of the war offering justifications for our presence which have little foundation in history, reason, law, or the course of events. Perhaps it is simply proof of the saying that in war truth is the first casualty. Most startling of all is the recent claim that the United States has a formal and binding commitment to use its armies to defend Vietnam—a commitment resting on the Southeast Asia Treaty, or, alternatively, on Presidential statements over more than a decade. Secretary Rusk himself testified, "It is this fundamental SEATO obligation that has from the outset guided our actions in Vietnam." The language of the treaty itself is imprecise. In case of "armed attack" we agreed only "to meet the common danger in accordance with [our] constitutional processes." No nation is specifically required to go to war, although it is true that a skilled lawyer could interpret the language as a commitment or as an excuse for inaction, depending upon his instructions. The conclusive fact, however, is that neither our fellow-signers, including France and Britain, nor John Foster Dulles, who drew up the treaty, nor any American President has believed or been advised that those words required us to send fighting men to Vietnam. Under close questioning by Senator Hickenlooper, who was eager to refute the slightest insinuation that this was "Ike's war," General Taylor admitted, "No, sir. Very clearly we made no such commitment. We didn't want such a commitment. This was the last thing we had in mind. . . . Insofar as the use of our combat ground forces are concerned, that [commitment] took place, of course, only in the spring of 1965." One can search the many statements of Presidents and diplomats in vain for any mention of the SEATO Treaty. Time after time, President Johnson set forth the reasons for our presence in Vietnam, but he never spoke of the requirements of the treaty, nor did anyone at the State Department suggest that he should, even though they surely reviewed every draft statement. The treaty argument is, in truth, something a clever advocate conceived a few months ago.

The claim of a SEATO commitment is often buttressed by quotations from the American Presidents concerned—Eisenhower, Kennedy, and Johnson—used to attribute to them the pledge that, in President Kennedy's words, the Communists shall not win "for lack of any support which the United States might render." But for every statement of this kind there is another, such as the one in the Kennedy interview of September, 1963, cautiously warning that "we can help them, we can give them equipment, we can send our men out there as advisers, but they have to win it—the people of Vietnam." President Johnson repeated many times the same careful limitation on American involvement. It is unfortunate that the demands of the modern Presidency require such an enormous, unending flood of words and speeches, inevitably resulting in imprecise and ambiguous language. The meaning rests not on a word-by-word analysis of an old text but on the common assumptions and realities of their setting. No President committed American combat troops to Vietnam before they actually went. No President believed he had made such a commitment. No one ever thought he had. No adviser in the highest councils ever urged action on the basis of the SEATO Treaty or of any other pledge; none, as far as I know, ever mentioned the existence of such a pledge. And, in fact, there was no such commitment. Combat troops were sent because our national interest, in the judgment of our leaders, required their presence, and for no other reason.

Efforts to justify our presence in Vietnam by elevating it to the grand scale of a decisive "testing ground for the war of liberation," of "another Munich," or of the beginning of a fall of "dominoes" are equally unnecessary and also defective. In large part, the struggle in Vietnam is indeed a war of internal aggression—what Soviet and Chinese leaders call a "war of liberation." It certainly is not the decisive one. Win or lose, we will face similar challenges, just as our success in Greece and Turkey was followed, much later, by Soviet intervention in Cuba. Invasion in Korea was halted, and Quemoy and Matsu were bombarded. Firmness in the Formosa Strait did not halt efforts at subversion in places as remote as the Congo and the Central African Republic. Fighting in Malaya and the Philippines and on the Indian border came to an end, but fighting continues in Vietnam. This war is another episode—a particularly dangerous and bloody one—in a long, continuing conflict. General Taylor has already informed us that "they are beginning in Thailand." Nor is this the Asian equivalent of the decision at Munich. There the Allies yielded to a nation with a timetable for the armed conquest of Europe. Moreover, it is unlikely in the extreme that a firm stand at Munich would have long halted a madman armed with the best military machine in Europe. It might have changed the terms and timing of war but not war itself. Had the time the Allies bought been used to prepare, Munich might be now considered an act of statesmanship. Our refusal to yield in Vietnam stands on its own merits, not on those of a distant and indistinct analogy. Nor would the simple fact of Communist rule set a row of dominoes falling. In 1949, the biggest domino of all, China, fell, and others did not follow. It is the fact of American defeat, the demonstration of American futility, rather than the presence of a Communist government in Vietnam, that would shake uncertain governments in Asia.

The American war in Vietnam flows not from

formal commitment or historical theory but from the history of this cruel and confused conflict. The effort to rewrite that history only bewilders the supporters and strengthens the opponents of government policy in Vietnam, carrying the debate into irrelevant dead ends of discussion and contradiction.

The Vietnamese war is twenty years old. It began while Chiang Kai-shek still ruled China and the French owned Indo-China. On September 2, 1945, Ho Chi Minh issued the Vietnamese Declaration of Independence: "All men are created equal. They are endowed by their Creator with certain unalienable rights, and among these are life, liberty, and the pursuit of happiness." On the evening of December 19th, of the next year, city streets all over Vietnam were instantly cloaked in night by a coordinated attack on power stations across the country. The war had begun. It was first ignored, then shared, by the United States, which gave more than a billion dollars of aid to the beleaguered French. Early in 1954, John Foster Dulles announced that the new French military policy was designed to "break the organized body of Communist aggression by the end of the 1955 fighting season." But in May, 1954, before that fighting season came, the great powers assembled at Geneva to work out the terms of a French defeat. The Geneva

Conference granted Vietnam independence, prohibited it from forming military alliances or accommodating foreign bases, guaranteed it democratic freedoms, and divided the country into North and South until national elections could be held in 1956, making it clear that the partition was "provisional" and "should not in any way be interpreted as constituting a political or territorial boundary."

At this point, accounts and histories, claims and charges trail off into uncertainty and illusion. The course and nature of the "second" Vietnamese war are cloaked in ignorance, obscured by the diverging views of historians, buried in the archives of Hanoi, Peking, the State Department, and the Quai d'Orsay, interred with the bodies of Diem and his brother.

We do know, however, that the new, semi-official narrative of straightforward Communist duplicity and aggression does not tell the whole story. According to Secretary Rusk, the Communists violated the Geneva agreement at the very beginning by leaving a hard core of agents in the South. Yet the International Control Commission, including friendly and responsive Canada, found in 1955 that "the provisions of . . . a military or semi-military nature have on the whole been carried out." It is true that some agents were left. Most of the five thousand guerrillas still to be found in South Vietnam were South Vietnamese who had gone home, as they were entitled to do. Then, we are told, during the next five years Hanoi "developed a secret political-military organization in the South," conducted a campaign of terror and assassination, and, like a "typical police state," refused to let the national elections scheduled for 1956 be held. This refusal is surely the greatest political self-denial in history, since President Eisenhower has estimated that "possibly eighty per cent of the population [of all Vietnam] would have voted for the Communist Ho Chi Minh." In the late fifties, the new narrative goes on, North Vietnam began to infiltrate the South with "disciplined adherents whom the Party [had] ordered North at the time of the settlement," and directed them to "form cadres around which guerrilla units could be built." Finally, in 1960, Hanoi created the National Liberation Front, to serve as a "political façade" for the conquest of a people enjoying "substantial progress" under Diem. Infiltration increased. The Army of North Vietnam joined the battle. And here we are.

The whole of this careful structure, faintly reminiscent of an entry in the Soviet Encyclopedia concerning the American contribution to the Second World War, is designed to prove that the struggle in Vietnam is solely "a systematic aggression by Hanoi against the people of South Vietnam." Some of this account is accurate and some of it is distorted. More often events are described with a certainty and simplicity that do not exist. On February 3rd, Vice-President Hubert Humphrey was more candid about the complexities, telling a New York audience, "Some of these revolutionaries are from the South. Some are from the North. Some are irregulars. Some are regular North Vietnamese soldiers. Some of their supply and direction comes from the South. Some of it comes from Hanoi. Some of it comes from Peking." The President said, more compactly, "Some of the people of South Vietnam are participating in attack on their own government." The reality is that there is aggression and there is also civil war. Some of the revolutionaries are Communists and some are not. Some wish to associate with China and others are passionate nationalists.

From 1954 until 1956, North Vietnam for the most part bided its time, expecting that South Vietnam would soon be under its control. When the time came for the elections required by the treaty, President Diem, with encouragement from the United States, refused to hold them—because he rightly feared defeat—and began a rigorously severe repression against his political enemies, including the small number of Communists who, along with other dissidents, were seeking a foothold in the countryside. Spurred by this repression, by the desire to overthrow Diem, by the failure to hold elections, and by a small but growing amount of help from the North, the revolutionaries organized. They began to terrorize the peasants, propagandize the villages, and even carry out a few small measures of reform. Nor did Diem improve relations by creating, in 1958, a Committee for the Liberation of North Vietnam, which parachuted agents into Northern areas of discontent, or by refusing to trade badly needed rice. Finally, in 1960, Hanoi called for a National Liberation Front to lead the growing struggle in the South—an organization whose "nominal leader," according to Vice-President Humphrey, "is not known as a Communist"— which is clearly responsive to Hanoi but whose exact relationship, puppet or partly independent, is certainly unknown and probably mixed.

By 1960, fifteen village chiefs a week were being killed by revolutionaries. Infiltration from the North was on the rise. Today, as the President has said, the support and direction from the North are "the heartbeat of the war." But the war never was, and is not now, only a war of North against South. Secretary McNamara carefully explained in 1964 that even though Northern support and direction are "a critical factor . . . the large indigenous support that the Vietcong receives means that solutions must be as political and economic as military," and he added, "Indeed, there can be no such thing as a purely 'military' solution." This appraisal is strengthened by the Defense Department estimate that of a total of about three hundred and thirty thousand Vietcong, dead and alive, only sixty-three thousand have been infiltrators. More than a quarter million have been recruited from among the people who live in the South. Our enemies are not only ruthless aggressors and assassins but also men like Do Luc, whose diary, found on his body, contains the lines "Leaving temporarily the beloved North to return to my native South to liberate my compatriots from the yoke of misery imposed by My-Diem [U.S. Diem]. . . . Now my life is full of hardship, not enough rice to eat, not enough salt to give a taste to my tongue, not enough clothing to keep myself warm! But in my heart I keep loyal to the Party and to the people. I am proud and happy."

Neither the country nor the President is served by a reduction of the confused and blending tones of history to sharp blacks and whites. President Johnson, with clearer insight, has spoken of "the confused nature of this conflict." It is enough to know, without seeking a consistent and deliberate plot stretching over a dozen years, that there is aggression—in Johnson's words, "an attack by one country on another." Yet at the same time there is also civil war, discontent, unfulfilled aspirations, and violent passions among the people of the South. Any effort at a political solution must take shape from that reality as well, if it is to be accepted or if, once accepted, it is to endure.

Just as our immense and dangerous involvement in this confused conflict does not rest on formal commitment or on resistance to "simple aggression," it did not emerge from a clear and consistent policy, based on a clear consciousness, at every step, of the implications, dangers, and possibilities of the future. As in many great national enterprises, each individual decision seemed reasonable, carefully limited, even necessary. We looked cautiously ahead while the door closed slowly, ponderously behind us.

More important than any other single factor was the hopeful expectation, the wish, deeply grounded in the American character, that victory might come easily and with little pain. In 1954, Eisenhower wrote a letter offering to "examine" a program of aid if needed reforms were carried out in South Vietnam. The object was to build a stable country that could stand on its own feet—nothing more than we were doing, and still are doing, in dozens of countries. In 1955, a few soldiers crossed the Pacific to help train the South Vietnamese Army to do a better job of protecting its own country; this training mission was similar to the missions we have in other parts of Asia and in many countries of South America. Nevertheless, the United States slowly began to replace the French as the dominant foreign power in a weak, unstable, menaced land. Next, as terror and attack mounted—though still on a small scale—under President Kennedy, the American military presence began to increase. It consisted of advisers, instructed to train, help, counsel, but not to fight. Late in 1961, we suffered our first military casualty. By the end of that year, there were three thousand American troops in South Vietnam; by the end of the next year, eleven thousand; by the end of 1963, sixteen thousand.

At every step, it seemed to many that the struggle was almost won. Who, in good conscience, and in the interests of the United States, could refuse the small additional help that did not seem to risk major conflict yet might prevent a Communist takeover? In March, 1963, our commander in Vietnam, General Paul Harkins, assured the nation, and the President, that the South Vietnamese armed forces "had all that was required for victory." That October, Secretary of Defense McNamara and General Taylor announced that "the major part of the U.S. military task can be completed by the end of 1965." A month later, General Harkins prophesied, even more glowingly, that "victory is . . . just months away." And in the secret meetings of the National Security Council the reports, estimates, and counsel were still more optimistic and assured, although a few advisers were more skeptical. These were the judgments of men of intelligence and force. Robert McNamara is a most brilliant Secretary of Defense and a principal voice of restraint in the administration; Maxwell Taylor is among the most thoughtful and enlightened of generals. The shifting group around the conference table was one of the most luminous ever assembled in government. Why were the estimates so faulty? In part, of course, they were not. The enemy forces were relatively small. The South Vietnamese Army was growing in power and effectiveness. But the reasonable, even brilliant military calculations masked a whole series of erroneous political assumptions. The crucial variables in the equation of victory were not firepower or troops but the will of the Vietcong to fight, the strength and stability of the South Vietnamese government, the intentions and capacities of North Vietnam. As it turned out, the Vietcong were more determined, and had greater local support, than we thought; the South Vietnamese military was less effective and its government (soon to be tumbled in a flood of popular discontent) weaker than we thought; North Vietnam was more willing to take risks and better equipped to make war. The estimates were reasoned, but they were based on the wrong evidence or on evidence that was far more uncertain than anyone believed. Added to these critical misjudgments were a certain amount of wishful thinking and, more important, the fact that other problems—Cuba and Berlin and the test-ban treaty—were clamoring for attention. Had we more precisely judged what the future might bring, the same decisions might still have been made, but they would have been made with a clearer awareness of onrushing danger.

In 1964, the process continued, assisted and complicated by President Johnson's need to assert his new leadership, map out a program, and prepare for election. We continued to "advise and help," although more of those concerned began to see the dimensions of the approaching crisis. Finally, early in 1965, the President was advised that morale in South Vietnam could be revived only if we bombed military targets in North Vietnam. This would assure Saigon of our determination to stay the course, and perhaps, if we were lucky, would so weaken Hanoi's will to fight that we could avoid the unpleasant, looming need to send in large numbers of combat troops. Thus the most fateful decision of all was made. The war went North. What had been an important but subdued conflict became a major international crisis. In the election of 1964, although Vietnam was occasionally mentioned, not a single complete speech of President Johnson's was devoted to that conflict. (We did not then refer to it as a war.) Opinion polls commissioned by local candidates and the national Democratic Party showed that as few as four or five per cent of the people in many states considered it an issue of major concern; it was ranked distantly behind unemployment, disarmament, and even Cuba. From the day of the bombing, however, Vietnam, rapidly swallowing up all other concerns and dangers, was never to leave the front pages of the world.

By the spring of 1965, it was clear that if American combat troops, in large numbers, did not enter the war, defeat was not only likely but imminent. "Early in 1965 . . . it was widely felt on both sides . . . that it was only a matter of time before the Communists would win, unless something was done about it," McGeorge Bundy said in February. After the most painful discussion, a commitment of combat troops was made, limited only by developing military needs, and Vietnam became an irrevocably American war.

Flowing from the cruel necessities of the present, informed by awareness of the past, is the third Vietnam debate: the passionate unresolved clash about the future. Thousands of lives are at hazard, and there are rising risks of war with the entire three-hundred-thousand-man Army of North Vietnam, of a titanic conflict with the legions of China, and even, in ultimate—decisive—holocaust, of armed conflict with the Soviet Union.

President Johnson, guided by the information he receives, confined and influenced by advisers, swayed by opinion, coerced by events, directed by national tradition and principle, nevertheless holds the vital decisions in his hands alone. Alarmed at this enormous power, some people have denied its existence. "This President of ours cannot justify under the Constitution sending a single American boy to . . . South Vietnam without a declaration of war," Senator Morse said at the hearings. "We are involved illegally in this war." A President's power to involve the country in armed conflict—argued and indecisively compromised at the Constitutional Convention—has been resolved by history. President Polk knowingly brought on the Mexican War by ordering American troops into an area disputed with Mexico (although war was later declared). In 1861, Lincoln established an armed blockade of Southern ports when Congress was not yet in session. Theodore Roosevelt openly boasted, "I took Panama." Truman sent troops to Korea, and Eisenhower to Lebanon, without asking Congress. Kennedy approved the Bay of Pigs invasion and commanded the armed blockade of Cuba on his own. Today, the congressional power to declare war is little more than a ratification of events and acts already past. Congress can censure Presidential action, or even cripple it by refusing to vote money or troops. But this is not being done, partly because many congressmen support the war, partly because others follow the reasoning attributed by Benjamin Thomas to Representative Abraham Lincoln during the Mexican War—that even though he opposed the war, "whenever supply bills were presented, he, like most other Whigs, voted for them rather than risk popular disfavor." Lincoln himself, his political career seemingly devastated by open opposition to the Mexican War, explained to William Herndon, in terms that might appeal to many men now in Congress, "The Locos are untiring in their efforts to make the impression that all who vote supplies . . . do of necessity approve the President's conduct in the beginning of it; but the Whigs from the beginning made and kept the distinction between the two."

It is not possible to convey the full flavor of a meeting of final resolution conducted by Lyndon Johnson. In the early summer of 1965, following several days of discussion, the President and his advisers—Rusk, McNamara, Bundy, Director of the

Central Intelligence Agency William Raborn, Chairman of the Joint Chiefs of Staff General Earle Wheeler, Under-Secretary of State George Ball, and several Presidential assistants—met to discuss the decision that he intended to announce the next morning. It was already clear that combat troops would be sent to Vietnam. The question was whether the reserves should be summoned, a national emergency declared, and the nation given a serious war warning. Throughout the debate, the President sat slouched and almost unnoticed in his chair, listening, and asking questions. As debate trailed off, he sat upright, the massive physical presence suddenly dominating the table. "Gentlemen," he said, "here are the alternatives." He carefully listed five choices, the last being to commit only the troops then needed, without calling the reserves. His tone left little doubt of his own choice. He then went back over the alternatives, pausing after each one to ask, unsmiling, "Does anyone favor that?" As No. 4, the most drastic, met the same silence as the others, he turned and, staring at the Chairman of the Joint Chiefs of Staff, rose without putting the fifth, and favored, choice, said "Thank you, gentlemen," and left.

During the night, the President personally inserted in his announcement the most advanced peace proposals we had made—free elections, reunification if this should be voted, a cease-fire, and a clear willingness to hear the Vietcong at the conference table—at one stroke overriding long-held objections. Few incidents better dramatized the painful, consistent Presidential desire to prevent defeat while resisting proposals to enlarge the conflict beyond what the present seemed to demand. The wisdom of such a course can be debated, but I do not doubt Lyndon Johnson's desire to end the war. It is killing Americans and threatening the death of many more. It has already reduced resources for education and housing, for conservation and the war against poverty. It is endangering our prosperity. It is, far more than is yet clear, seriously weakening national support for the Democratic Party and the President himself. The depth of this possible disaffection is hinted at by the recent Gallup poll showing that sixty-seven per cent of the people would favor a congressional candidate who advocated that we "try harder to reach a compromise peace settlement." (Fifteen per cent would oppose such a candidate; eighteen per cent had no opinion.)

But how can the war be ended? On that issue, the public record reveals, there is a real and danger-filled clash—unresolved, barely articulated, and now in process of decision. Few wish either withdrawal or what the President called "mindless escalation," involving an immediate devastation of North Vietnam or an attack on China. These views have no serious prospects, at least for the moment. There are, rather, two middle grounds, presenting different risks, and leading in different directions. On one side are those who believe we should fight a carefully limited war, restricted to combat in South Vietnam and pacification of the countryside; that we should refuse to expand, and perhaps even reduce or halt, the bombing of the North; and that we should aggressively seek a compromise political settlement, with the inevitably uncertain risk that the Communists might ultimately win control of the country. On the other side are those who wish to use all the military power needed, in the North as well as in the South, to bring the Vietcong to their knees and break the will of Hanoi to continue the war—who wish to compel the Communists into an unfavorable political settlement or no settlement at all. "I don't think anybody suggests literally exterminating them," General Taylor testified, "but we would like to have them so beaten that they would be glad to come in and accept an amnesty." Our policy today rests precariously on the first alternative—carefully limited conflict, leading to a fair, if risky, compromise. However, the pressures of circumstances and events are urging us imperceptibly toward the second course, exposing us to the steadily enlarging danger of a course that has no logical and certain end except in measureless rivers of blood.

Our future policy in Vietnam must follow two parallel roads—the road of negotiation and the road of combat. Past miscalculation should have humbled us to the awareness that each specific step may have larger consequences than we can foresee. Each should be tested against a single standard: Does it serve or injure the bedrock vital interest of the United States? That interest is to establish that American military power, once committed to defend another nation, cannot be driven from the field. It is not to guarantee South Vietnam forever against the possibility of a Communist takeover.

Hanoi's unwillingness to negotiate is one of the great mysteries of the war. At best, negotiation would give them a favorable result; at worst, negotiation would make it almost impossible for the United States—compelled to show good faith at the conference table—to step up the war. In fact, some of the more militant members of the Washington community have expressed fearful apprehension lest our offer be accepted. The answer to the mystery is buried in the unknown calculations of enemy leaders, the internal politics of North Vietnam, the obscure relations among the Vietcong, Hanoi, Peking, and Moscow. Certainly North Vietnam can no longer hope for victory, either by force of arms or by the failure of will. Yet perhaps it does, knowing so little about the strange stubbornness, streaked with violence, of the American mind. Recent proofs of instability and division in South Vietnam may add fuel to that hope. Probably the North Vietnamese also suspect that we are asking them to the negotiating table simply to compel their surrender, that nothing we have yet said assures an acceptable compromise, and that if they talk without such assurance it will destroy the morale of the thousands of guerrillas who have undergone years of cruel hardship and danger. Beyond this is Peking, urging, demanding, warning against discussions, establishing its own direct relations with the Vietcong over the head of Hanoi, seemingly delighted to see Americans involved—without cost to China, though not without risk—in a war that helps feed its hope of wresting world Communist leadership from the Soviet Union.

We have had, as we are often reminded, many communications with Hanoi. The critical question, however, is not how many times we have talked but what we have said, not how many notes we have sent but what they have contained. We cannot know this with certainty, but the vagueness of public discussion strengthens a general conviction that the terms of a realistic political settlement have not yet been communicated—a conviction that is further supported by the suggestion of U Thant, expressed in a January interview with a reliable correspondent for the Washington *Post*, that *"as a next step* . . . concrete proposals be made on what type of government in South Vietnam, representative, as far as possible, of all the sections of the South Vietnamese people . . . could take over the responsibility of organizing the exercise by the people of the right to decide their own affairs." Clearly, such proposals must answer at least three basic questions. First, who will shape the terms of settlement? Certainly Hanoi cannot come to the table if the Vietcong, who bear the burden of combat, are excluded. Even if it could, to do so would require its admission that the war of liberation in South Vietnam was "simple aggression," that it had consistently lied to the world. Its own very recent claim that the Vietcong are "the sole legitimate representative" of South Vietnam is surely a response to our own assertions that the Vietcong are, in the Vice-President's words, but a "stooge," an "agent," of Hanoi. Stripped of pejoratives, however, our current utterances seem to express willingness to talk to the Vietcong. There is, the President said, "no insuperable problem" to having the Vietcong's views represented at a conference. Ambassador Averell Harriman elaborated this when he said that the Vietcong can come either "as part of the North Vietnamese delegation or as an independent group . . . but not as a government." The paper-thin problem of formal labels is no formidable barrier to those who really want to talk. The second, and most important, of the three questions concerns the makeup of the ultimate government of Vietnam. We are willing to see "free elections" in which the Communists can organize, can campaign, and perhaps can win a voice in government. If this happens—and the popular support of the Vietcong makes it likely that it will—we will "honor their result." Once there is peace, we will support a neutral South Vietnam, without military alliances or foreign bases, and free to choose whether or not to reunite with the Communist North. So, according to their published program, will the Vietcong. The third question has to do with the governing of Vietnam between a final settlement and elections. In a country as weak, unstable, and disorganized as Vietnam, elections will be confused, difficult, and disputed. Clearly, we cannot trust the Communists to run free elections. Nor can they be reasonably expected to rely on the honesty and dispassion of General Ky (or his successor). If elections are to mean anything, the country must be directed in this interim period by a compromise government, trusted by both sides, their trust being supported by an effective network of international guarantees, by international supervision, or even by an international armed force sufficient to prevent a repetition of the 1956 refusal to hold elections (made possible, at least in part, by the withdrawal of French forces at the request of Diem). This may mean that some Communists will be allowed to share in the interim government. It may mean a government of Buddhists and neutrals, or even an international trusteeship. There are many in South Vietnam well suited to such a role; the vital matter is the international guarantees and international forces that will insure both free elections and peaceful accession by the victors.

This *sine qua non* of a negotiated settlement was at the center of the confused debate that raged over the February 19th statement of Senator Kennedy— a debate that dramatized the impossibility of publicly discussing complex issues, especially amid the intricacies of high politics. Kennedy stated that an acceptable compromise would involve "a share of power and responsibility" for the Vietcong, shaped to avoid the possibility of "domination or internal conquest," with "international guarantees to back up agreement," while the political process would be placed "under the rigorous supervision of a trusted international body." Our willingness to accept the "uncertainties of election" would be matched by a clear demonstration that we would not permit conquest by force. The record of debate does not sustain the impression that Kennedy withdrew from this position in the fire that followed. There were, however, misreadings, followed by attacks on the proposals as thus interpreted. In fact, he did little more than elaborate what Senator Fulbright had said unnoticed to Secretary Rusk the day before: "I do not recall . . . we have ever made it crystal clear that we will support an election supervised by an appropriate international body, and that we will accept the results. . . . It is also not clear that we are willing to allow any participation of the National Liberation Front either in a provisional government or at any time and, therefore, there is no alternative for them but surrender or annihilation." When the cannonade of comment is sifted, and then stripped of imprecations, accusations, zeal to be in the front ranks of anti-Communism, and the fervent but always risky effort to read the unspoken thoughts of the President, the discussion does not seem to leave the administration position far from this. But the debate did, for just a moment, throw a ray of light on inner differences of temperament and attitude. It seemed that Secretary Rusk closed the door when, the day before the Kennedy statement, in answer to Fulbright's dogged pursuit of the alternative to the "possibility of participation" by the Vietcong, he said, "They do have an alternative. They are the front of Hanoi. They do have an alternative of quitting, of stopping being an agent of Hanoi and receiving men and arms from the North." McGeorge Bundy added to the confusion two days later by asserting, "The administration does not take the view that admitting the Communists to a share of power and responsibility would be a useful or helpful step," and then, lapsing into the most painful possible rejoinder, quoted President Kennedy against his brother on the wholly irrelevant problem of popular fronts in Europe. (Closer to the problem—if past heroes are to be invoked—is President Kennedy's response to a question about the dangers of coalition government in Laos: "We are taking a chance in all of Southeast Asia. . . . I can assure you that I recognize the risks that are involved. But I also think that we should consider the risks if we fail, and particularly of the possibility of escalation of a military struggle in a place of danger.") Once the verbal torrent diminished, it was clear that the President had not embraced the Bundy view. In public speeches and press conferences, he carefully avoided saying anything against the approach of Fulbright and Kennedy. We would "honor the result" of an election, the President said—presumably even if the Communists should win. And the makeup of an interim government, according to Ambassador Arthur Goldberg and the White House, would "be left to the negotiating parties"—which keeps the door open for compromise. The structure of such a compromise (or the many possible variants of compromise) and our willingness to communicate specific proposals to Hanoi are left to future actions and decisions.

Is there a possibility of such a settlement? Hanoi has proposed four points for negotiation. Secretary Rusk, in setting forth fourteen points of his own, said that "the effect of those four points . . . would be to give away the very purposes for which we are fighting and to deliver the people of South Vietnam against their will to the domination of a Communist regime." Yet the substance, if not the intention, of the four points is not impossibly distant from the Secretary's own program. It is generally agreed that only the third point, calling for a settlement of the affairs of South Vietnam "in accordance with the program of the National Liberation Front," is totally unacceptable. Although that program has shifted over the years, its essentials have remained constant. Once past the unflattering references to "gangster-style U.S. culture," it calls, in its fullest 1961 version, for "a new constitution," "a new National Assembly through universal suffrage," "all democratic liberties" (including freedom of speech and worship), land reform through "purchase from landowners," "a foreign policy of peace and neutrality," the elimination of all foreign military bases, close unity with "peace-loving and neutral countries" (first of all, with "neighboring Cambodia and Laos"), the overthrow of the Diem regime (since accomplished), and the establishment of "a national democratic" coalition administration, and so on. Of course, there are hidden traps and dangerous ambiguities, such as a granting of freedom only to "patriotic" political parties, a call for reunification by negotiations rather than through elections (although the negotiating government would be elected, and although this year Hanoi proposed reunification through elections), and an absence of international guarantees for elections. It would be naïve to think that the program was not intended to move toward a Communist takeover. Yet in the main, when the ritual curses have been excised, Hanoi's four points, including the Front program, sound much like ours; the expressed differences are no greater than those in many productive Cold War negotiations. Perhaps this is all propaganda; perhaps victory, not settlement, is the real goal. Yet, whatever Hanoi's reaction, the time has come for the United States to formulate a fair and detailed outline of settlement. Of course, we cannot, as George Ball has said, "first

announce it to a television audience and then . . .
sit down at a bargaining table." Fruitful discussion
will begin in secrecy, where it can be free from
political pressures, from critics, and from the cor-
rosive compulsion toward simplicity which marks
public debate. The essentials are there: a cease-fire,
a laying down of arms so that the entire country can
be governed, and an end to bombing; a structure
to guarantee elections and also peaceful accession
by the victors; a withdrawal of foreign forces, and
neutralization; free elections, with Communist participation. Such proposals, couched in the most
specific possible terms, should be communicated to
Hanoi, accompanied or quickly followed by a meeting between a high United States official and a top
North Vietnamese. Negotiations, even in the lofty
chambers of international politics, cannot be conducted successfully by notes and messengers. Only
men confident of their authority and their ability,
and fully aware of the implications of their own
proposals and the proposals of others—in other
words, no more than half a dozen men in America
—can hope to bring such negotiations to a successful conclusion, or even bring an accurate account of them to the President.

It does not illuminate reality to say, as some
have said, that we cannot "dictate to South Vietnam" what form a settlement should take. It is not

conceivable that the United States should continue a major war simply because the temporary chieftain in Saigon did not agree with our position. Nor can any South Vietnamese leader hope to withstand determined American pressure toward a settlement.

In the inevitable political instability of a peaceful South Vietnam, there is always a risk that the Communists may ultimately win political power—that the fox may insinuate its way, or be voted, into the chicken coop. It is this danger that stiffens some people's resistance to negotiations. It would indeed be an unfortunate outcome, but, measured by our vital interest—avoiding military defeat—it would not be fatal. It is no more than the chance we are constantly taking all across the world in Cold War competition. The only way to compel the Vietcong to a settlement that does not involve such a risk is to crush them in battle.

That battle now goes on in two wars, separated by the Seventeenth Parallel—the war in the North and the war in the South. The Northern war carries a far more grave danger of a larger, bloodier, and increasingly devastating struggle. On the objectives of the war there has been a subtle change of direction among many of those responsible for its conduct. Less than a year ago, our objective was "a stalemate." Once the guerrillas were convinced that victory was impossible, they would come to the conference table. Now important voices, publicly and privately, are lifted in favor not of a standoff but of victory. On March 3rd, Secretary McNamara told a Senate committee, "We win if North Vietnam leaves South Vietnam alone [translated: if the Vietcong stop fighting]. . . . We believe we can win in the sense I indicated." Two weeks earlier, on February 17th, General Taylor testified that the time to negotiate is not "until it is quite clear their course of action is a losing one"—a flat contradiction, as Senator Aiken reminded the General, of the President's expressed desire to negotiate now. Other officials are proclaiming it our intention to "destroy" major enemy units, or to break Hanoi's "will to fight." It is a mistake to read too much into individual statements and speeches, plucked out of the careless and ceaseless verbal flow of official Washington, but the absence of contradiction, the growing lack of caution, the obviously planted news stories, and the other evidence charged with significance for the insider (an official in the highest ranks of foreign policy said that the *Life* article called "Vietnam: The War Is Worth Winning" was one of the most helpful he had seen) all strongly indicate that a substantial section of the community of power believes that military victory is our principal, perhaps our only, objective. I myself am convinced that this belief is growing, but it is significant, and heartening, that the President has not called for armed triumph.

Victory in the South may be possible, with the major Communist units destroyed or broken up, morale shattered, and the guerrillas laying down their arms, asking for amnesty, or peacefully returning to their homes. We are, after all, killing greater and greater numbers of Vietcong. One high official estimates that the "kill rate" may average a thousand a week throughout the year. (Like nearly all the statistics of this war, such an estimate is necessarily flawed by doubts and inadequate information.) The defection rate is increasing, too (now at a weekly average of three to four hundred), although it does not yet match desertions from the South Vietnamese Army. Areas that once provided the guerrillas with secure sanctuary are now constantly menaced by descending helicopters and mobile troops. Yet many heavy clouds obscure the view toward "victory." Past misjudgments impose a fierce skepticism about promises—however faint and tentative—of military triumph. Since the early nineteen-fifties, they have always been wrong. Recently, we were told that the "tide" was turning—a phrase that accidentally echoed the Pentagon pronouncement of May, 1963, that "the corner definitely has been turned" toward victory. In 1962, McNamara said that the "ratio of killed and captured" was much more favorable; while a year later General Harkins proclaimed encouragingly from Saigon, "The Vietcong are losing because we are steadily decreasing their areas of maneuver and the terrain over which they can move at will." With a change in dates, these statements would fit unnoticed into many of today's briefings and releases. It is natural for men whose business is to fight wars to believe they can win, just as any good politician secretly believes he can win an election no matter how unfavorable the odds. Past mistakes are no guarantee of future error. There is a possibility that they may be right this time, but history teaches a reluctance to hazard great things on such predictions.

Moreover, it is unclear what victory means. The Secretary of State has said that our only commitment is to stop armed attack from the North—that if the North Vietnamese "were to show the slightest interest in withdrawing their regular armed forces and infiltrators, we could move to peace very quickly and the United States could withdraw its forces." How easy it is to become captive of the incomplete view that the Vietcong are "simply . . . the military arm of North Vietnam." A withdrawal of all infiltrators would leave more than a hundred thousand trained guerrillas in South Vietnam, and there would be no certainty that

Hanoi could completely stop the fighting or that such an order, if it should be obeyed at first, would not soon be ignored. Unless a negotiated settlement gives the dissidents a role in the political life of the country, a peaceful outlet for their ambitions, hopes, and protests, we must remain—as well we may—occupiers for many years. That possibility, resting on uncertainty about the nature of a victorious or independent South Vietnam, is further strengthened by today's still unsettled turbulence. The demonstrations, many of them conducted by young men who have never lived in a country free of terror, civil strife, and the cruelties of war, remind us that the last few months of political quiet in South Vietnam were a rare interlude. To the extent that Communists have inspired division, the anti-government protests show alarming influence in cities we have long claimed to control. To the extent that they flow from local discontent, they reflect division about the future of South Vietnam and weariness with war, and indicate the mounting price in anti-American feeling we must inevitably pay for the growing weight of the American presence in that tiny land. Whatever the outcome, however, unless events sweep away our influence altogether, it is unlikely we will permit any government to come to power which would inflict on us what some would see as the "humiliation" of requesting our withdrawal.

Some people justify their optimism about victory in terms of "breaking the will" of the Communists to continue the fight. It is true that there are more and more defectors, and that prisoners arrive more and more tired, dejected, and hungry. But the battle goes on; despite our growing force, Hanoi seems more militant, and infiltration seems to be increasing as our own numbers increase. We cannot know the will of men we do not understand. From Thermopylae to the Japanese-infested islands of the Pacific and Hitler's Berlin bunker, history is full of individuals and fighting forces who chose to fight against impossible odds and accept certain death. Nor can we measure the determination of an aging Communist leader who has been waging war for almost a quarter of a century. It is a guess built on an assumption resting on a hope. Aggressors though they are, many of the Vietcong believe they are enlisted in the ranks of justice. Mai Xuan Phong wrote in his diary, "The most precious thing for a man is his life. . . . My whole life, my whole strength have been devoted to the most elevated and the most beautiful cause—the struggle for the liberation of mankind." The demonstrations in South Vietnam show either an increasing weariness with the war on our side or a far greater Communist penetration of the cities than we have cared to admit. The Communists' will to fight may dissolve tomorrow, but one should not wager many American lives on it.

Even if we win countless battles, our victory will not be assured. Success in a guerrilla war, as our experts have repeatedly told us, is not measured simply in deaths and prisoners but, for the most part, in areas of the country pacified and population controlled. There is no clear proof that our control over the population is increasing. General Taylor, at one point in his testimony, indicated that sixty per cent of the people were under friendly control instead of the fifty-three per cent of six months before. Other testimony shows this figure to be uncertain, probably unknown, or perhaps completely unjustified. Although the Vietcong controls fewer areas than before, there is no firm evidence that a single square mile has been "pacified"—that is, cleared of guerrillas, protected against future attack, and set on the road to economic improvement. Nor has the United States reached the end of its commitment. Our two hundred and thirty-five thousand men are, General Taylor admitted, "not sufficient." The probable conclusion—the simple arithmetic—of Secretary McNamara's March 3rd testimony before the Senate is that the United

States plans to have at least four hundred thousand troops in South Vietnam by the end of the year. They will be needed if we intend to keep up the offensive against enemy forces that can increase by eight thousand a month while we kill four thousand or less—and even this estimate of enemy increase rests on the highly speculative belief that no more supplies can be smuggled into the South than these troops require, or about a hundred and fifty tons a day. If we are wrong about this—and we may well be wrong—the number that can infiltrate could grow enormously, along with the number of our own troops. (We need four or five men for every enemy soldier, and South Vietnam is nearing the limit of its manpower.)

The hope of victory, however, is not just a harmless foible of some generals and their few State Department allies. It carries the enormous danger that in pursuit of that shining, elusive prize we will enlarge the war in the North. As the Southern conflict continues unabated, pressure for more aggressive attacks on North Vietnam will steadily mount—pressure from public opinion frustrated by an endless battle, pressure from politicians seeking to discredit the administration's will and courage, pressure from those still searching for that one untaken step which will bring success. I hope, and I believe, that the President will resist such pressure, for no one is more painfully aware than he of the immense hazards of enlarging the war in the North.

Since February 7, 1965, we have been bombing selected military targets in North Vietnam—roads and bridges, ammunition and supply dumps, and gathering points for guerrillas. The bombing began with the aim of restoring crumbling morale in South Vietnam and in the forlorn hope that North Vietnam, quaking under the punishing assault, would come to the conference table. Its present purpose, according to Deputy Secretary of Defense Cyrus Vance, is "to interdict the infiltration of men and material," or, as it is more expansively viewed by General Taylor, "In a very real sense, the objective of our air campaign is to change the will of the enemy leadership." There is little evidence that the bombing has either had serious effect on the flow of supplies or eroded the will of the North. Infiltration did increase during the pause in the bombing. It also increased before the pause and it has increased since, and we have no figures to prove that bombing has made any important difference. Bombing, it is claimed, imposes "a higher price" for infiltration. It is unclear what this means. The border between the two Vietnams is mostly jungle crossed by trails and waterways. The price of carrying supplies and of repairing roads and bridges is high in terms of human labor, but there are huge numbers of willing unemployed. The travel of men and supplies since the bombing is longer and more difficult, but the North Vietnamese have time and they are used to discomfort. Of course, the bombing has some effect, but there is no compelling public justification of these costly assaults on military grounds. General Matthew B. Ridgway, our commander in Korea—the last ground war in Asia—has concluded, "It is impossible to interdict the supply routes of an Asian army by air power alone. [In Korea] we had complete air mastery . . . we clobbered Chinese supply columns unmercifully. . . . But we did not halt their offensive nor materially diminish its strength."

The war in the North has neither halted aggression nor shattered the "will" of the enemy nor "punished Hanoi" beyond the limits of endurance, yet the Alice in Wonderland response of some is to call for a stepping up of the war. "We should go after more meaningful targets on a slow *progressive* scale," said General Taylor, a highly intelligent military moderate. This will, it is hoped, "provide a sobering reminder to the leaders in Hanoi that progressively they must pay a *mounting* price for the continuation of the support of the Vietcong insurgency."

The President has given a more restricted basis for the bombing—"to slow down aggression," "increase the confidence of . . . South Vietnam," and help "convince the leaders of North Vietnam—*and all who seek to share their conquest*—[that] we will not be defeated . . . grow tired . . . [or] withdraw." The bombing has helped strengthen Southern resolution, and it has also helped convince any reasonable adversary that armed conquest is inconceivable, though the combat troops we have sent to the South since the bombing began are a more compelling proof.

The objectives set forth by the President are limited ones, and they have largely been accomplished. However, the grander and more spacious desire to end the enemy's capacity for making war, destroy his will to fight, and punish him for wrongdoing opens limitless horizons of expansion. Moreover, this desire invokes judgments that are not military judgments. The will of a nation, the punishment it can take, the strength of national pride and feeling and resistance are not matters that military specialists or computers or the Rand Corporation can assess. They require an intimate knowledge of the culture and thought of alien lands and of obscurely known leaders. It may even be that, as a careful American study of the war against Germany indicated, bombing strengthens the fighting spirit of a people. A leading political figure recently said to me, "After all, if we were being bombed, we'd never give in." Even the purely military justification, unsupported by any civilian official, is insignificant, marginal, perhaps nonexistent. Should we destroy every fuel depot, power plant, and factory in sight, the necessary hundred and fifty tons of supplies could probably, with the help of Russia and China, be scraped together if the North Vietnamese were willing to sacrifice some of their urgent civilian needs. There is, of course, some chance that increasing the war in the North will force Hanoi to yield. Against this unsure speculation must be matched the fact that we can easily protect our vital national interst—avoiding military defeat or humiliation—by means of combat in the South, while also avoiding the soaring menace of wider war which attack on the North brings.

The belief that you must punish your enemy or break his will is insatiable. Every step that fails calls forth not an admission of miscalculation but a demand for something more. It is the whole history of this war. Now some people are asking us to mine the harbor at Haiphong, and thus threaten to destroy the ships of a dozen nations. In the background is the further demand that we wipe out port facilities, piers, and fuel dumps near civilian centers. Next will come power plants, water-storage areas, factories—the fruits of a decade of labor.

After that, the cities must go, for their destruction
will create chaos, topple the government, eliminate
the enemy. This process will not necessarily begin
—or, if it does, will not necessarily follow this
precise course. Yet it is a growing possibility. And
each step along this path will increase the danger of
a bigger war. Stalemate, compromise, or even defeat
in the South is probably tolerable to Hanoi and
Peking. They will live to fight another day. Increasing destruction in the North is another matter.
North Vietnam cannot stand idly by and accept
its own destruction. As we widen the net of
devastation—as the Northern "hostage" is shot—
the pressure on North Vietnam to send its three-
hundred-thousand-man Army into battle will
mount, thus calling a million and more Americans
into war. Nor can China easily watch in idleness
while we destroy North Vietnam; to do so would
wreck its claim to leadership in Asia and to the first
position among the Communist parties and nations.
If China intervenes, even on a limited scale, most
probably we will have to bomb her major facilities,
and even her cities. Certainly we would not fight
an unending torrent of Chinese soldiers in Southeast Asia; and there are, as the Secretary of State has
reminded us, "no more sanctuaries." Finally, there
is the dilemma of the Soviet Union in such a case,
forced to choose between China and America.

China may be hated and feared, but for Russia to permit its conquest or devastation by the United States would mean the end of the idea of world Communism. The rest can be left to the imagination.

I do not know whether any of this will happen if we extend the Northern war. No one knows. No one can predict with certainty the actions or intentions of other countries. Calculations of rational self-interest are not enough. Under-Secretary Ball said when he was asked about the possibility of Chinese intervention, "The decision . . . is going to be made in Peiping and not necessarily by the standards or reason or logic with which we are familiar." Those who remember Hitler's invasion of Russia might add that reason and logic of any kind are not always the controlling instruments for irrational man. However, this is the realistic range of hazard involved in the Northern war—a sober reminder, and a warning restraint on aggressive temptations and proposals.

The psychology of war makes it difficult to turn back—even from mistakes. The ability of people to accept and adjust to even the most horrifying realities means that continuing our present level of activity probably involves only a small increase in risk. Therefore, I should think a realistic as well as sound political-military strategy would draw a firm line at any further widening of the war in the North. It would do no harm—although it would be politically and psychologically difficult—to slow down or halt the present bombing of the North. It might be a good idea for the President to assure the nation that, in the absence of a major North Vietnamese attack, he intended to limit the war in this way. Such a speech would bring some minor comfort and relief to the enemy, but it would enormously ease the growing, restless apprehension that we may have embarked on a limitless course.

In the South, we have no choice but to continue the war. We are under attack, and withdrawal is impossible and unwise. Here we must commit the forces needed to hold our positions, erode the enemy ranks, and clear guerrillas from the countryside. The objective, however, should be not to crush the Vietcong in pursuit of an unlikely surrender but slowly to retake key areas of the country, mile by painful mile. Neither manpower nor money nor energy should be spared in the top-priority program of pacification. Once an area is conquered, garrisoned forces, if necessary, should assure continued security while we begin the work of social organization and economic investment, along with measures for education and the improvement of health, the harnessing of water power, and an increase in the yield of the land. If we now lack the

manpower for this most important task—and we do
—then both Americans and Vietnamese might well
be recruited, or even conscripted, for it. Such a
course might limit our battles and our deaths. It
would prove our determination far more effectively
than leaping across the country looking for guerrillas to kill, and would clearly demonstrate our
willingness to help build a sure base for a society
in which, to reverse Mao Tse-tung's famous image,
"the fish" of guerrilla armies cannot "swim." Here,
too, the President might well tell the American
people that the outcome is uncertain—that we may
turn a sudden corner and find victory but that it is
far more likely that we will see only a long, bloody,
inconclusive war of attrition, until returning sanity
brings a political settlement. For if the talk of victory is allowed to swell, the political consequences
of failure and the pressure to expand the war will
also mount.

Secretary Rusk, when he was asked by
Senator Pell if he saw any end to the "corridor we
are following," replied, "No; I would be misleading
you if I told you that I thought that I know where,
when, and how this matter will be resolved." A
few minutes later, he added, "The nature of a
struggle of this sort . . . is, of course, substantially
determined by the other side." Such a terrifying

admission of futility—an advance absolution—only conceals the truth that this enormous nation is not helplessly in the grip of events, that the future, like the past, will be shaped largely by our own judgments. It is easy, and it would be wrong, to be apocalyptic about a conflict that is still so strictly limited and so full of hopeful possibilities for settlement. We have emerged safe and strong from many equally dangerous enterprises. Yet not long ago an important politician, intimate with the processes of power, told me he thought that if large-scale war ever comes, it will come not in a burst of Strangelove madness or a Fail-Safe accident but through a long series of acts and decisions, each seemingly reasonable, that will slowly place the great powers in a situation in which they will find it impossible to back down. It will be no one's fault.

POSTSCRIPT

There was once a young king who conquered the world. At the very edge of civilization, he crossed a river to the lands of India and reached the far bank alone, amazed to see that his sullen army would not follow.

In the spring of 1966 it seemed, at times, that we might have the same experience in Vietnam; that a government might come to power that would end the war at the high risk of immediate Communist triumph. That possibility is now almost gone. Certainly the United States is devoting its considerable influence to preventing such an outcome; and large numbers of South Vietnamese, perhaps most of them, are unwilling to take that risk. Even those hostile to American presence are trapped between the imperatives of American power or Communist victory. Perhaps a future civilian government, if honest elections are held, can help find a middle way. Most probably the new government, like the old, will continue the war on the present basis. There is a chance, however, that a new government, while continuing the battle, will begin to make contact and carry on discussions with the leaders of the Vietcong, preparing the ground for their own negotiated solution. It would be well if we supported a government stable and self-confident enough to carry on this process. If there is to be a negotiated peace, it is more likely to be shaped between Vietnamese on both sides than among the United States, North Vietnam, and China. Such a result would flow from the almost forgotten truth that this is, or at least should be, an Asian war whose course and resolution are determined by Asians.

Meanwhile the war in the North continues its upward course. Targets are being expanded. Bombs now fall in the once sacrosanct Hanoi-Haiphong area. The great civilian centers are disturbed by the sound of explosives, and illuminated by the flames of incendiaries. In this way the danger of larger war continues to grow. The next large perilous stride will probably be signalled by a Communist counter-move, perhaps a sudden increase of infiltration or the use of Chinese planes to defend Hanoi against our bombers. (The Chinese have built air bases close to their border with North Vietnam.) Both inside the Administration and without there are an increasing number of responsible men—realists, hard-headed, experienced in government and diplomacy, supporters of our military efforts in Europe and Korea—who now believe

35831

we are moving closer to a huge conflict with North Vietnam, China, and even the Soviet Union.

Comment on the appearance of this essay in its original form revealed the ending to be more confusing than I had intended. "It will be no one's fault," but it will be the fault of many—leaders, politicians, journalists, men and women in a hundred different occupations in many lands who failed to see clearly, or act wisely, or speak articulately. There will be no act of madness, no single villain on whom to discharge guilt; just the flow of history.

The Geneva Conference on Indochina: Agreements and Declaration

[*The Geneva Conference on Indochina, attended by delegates from Great Britain and the U.S.S.R. (joint chairmen), France, the United States, Communist China, Cambodia, Laos, and Vietnam and the Viet Minh regime, lasted from May 8 until July 21, 1954. The terminating documents were the Agreement on the Cessation of Hostilities in Vietnam (not signed by the United States or Vietnam) and the Final Declaration of the Geneva Conference (adopted by a voice vote). In addition, the United States made a unilateral declaration of its position. This agreement ended the period of French colonial rule and set the stage for today's conflict. Both sides—Hanoi and Washington—have said they are prepared to return to at least the "essentials" of this agreement.*]

AGREEMENT ON THE CESSATION OF HOSTILITIES
IN VIETNAM *(July 20, 1954)*

Chapter I. Provisional Military Demarcation Line and Demilitarized Zone

1. A provisional military demarcation line shall be fixed, on either side of which the forces of the two parties shall be regrouped after their withdrawal, the forces of the People's Army of Vietnam [P.A.V., or Vietminh, forces] to the north of the line and the forces of the French Union to the south. . . .

It is also agreed that a demilitarized zone shall be established on either side of the demarcation line, to a width of not more than 5 kms. from it, to act as a buffer zone and avoid any incidents which might result in the resumption of hostilities.

2. The period within which the movement of all forces of either party into its regrouping zone on either side of the provisional military demarcation line shall be completed shall not exceed three hundred (300) days from the date of the present Agreement's entry into force.

3. When the provisional military demarcation line coincides with a waterway, the waters of such waterway shall be open to civil navigation by both parties wherever one bank is controlled by one party and the other bank by the other party. The Joint Commission shall establish rules of navigation for the stretch of waterway

in question. The merchant shipping and other civilian craft of each party shall have unrestricted access to the land under its military control.

4. The provisional military demarcation line between the two final regrouping zones is extended into the territorial waters by a line perpendicular to the general line of the coast.

All coastal islands north of this boundary shall be evacuated by the armed forces of the French Union, and all islands south of it shall be evacuated by the forces of the People's Army of Vietnam.

5. To avoid any incidents which might result in the resumption of hostilities, all military forces, supplies, and equipment shall be withdrawn from the demilitarized zone within twenty-five (25) days of the present Agreement's entry into force.

6. No person, military or civilian, shall be permitted to cross the provisional military demarcation line unless specifically authorized to do so by the Joint Commission.

7. No person, military or civilian, shall be permitted to enter the demilitarized zone except persons concerned with the conduct of civil administration and relief and persons specifically authorized to enter by the Joint Commission.

8. Civil administration and relief in the demilitarized zone on either side of the provisional military demarca-

tion line shall be the responsibility of the Commanders-in-Chief of the two parties in their respective zones. The number of persons, military or civilian, from each side who are permitted to enter the demilitarized zone for the conduct of civil administration and relief shall be determined by the respective Commanders, but in no case shall the total number authorized by either side exceed at any one time a figure to be determined by the Trung Gia Military Commission or by the Joint Commission. The number of civil police and the arms to be carried by them shall be determined by the Joint Commission. No one else shall carry arms unless specifically authorized to do so by the Joint Commission.

9. Nothing contained in this chapter shall be construed as limiting the complete freedom of movement—into, out of, or within the demilitarized zone—of the Joint Commission, its joint groups, the International Commission to be set up as indicated below, its inspection teams and any other persons, supplies, or equipment specifically authorized to enter the demilitarized zone by the Joint Commission. Freedom of movement shall be permitted across the territory under the military control of either side over any road or waterway which has to be taken between points within the demilitarized zone when such points are not connected by roads or waterways lying completely within the demilitarized zone.

Chapter II. Principles and Procedure Governing Implementation of the Present Agreement

10. The Commanders of the Forces on each side, on the one side the Commander-in-Chief of the French Union forces in Indochina and on the other side the Commander-in-Chief of the People's Army of Vietnam, shall order and enforce the complete cessation of all hostilities in Vietnam by all armed forces under their control, including all units and personnel of the ground, naval, and air forces.

11. In accordance with the principle of a simultaneous cease-fire throughout Indochina, the cessation of hostilities shall be simultaneous throughout all parts of Vietnam, in all areas of hostilities and for all the forces of the two parties. . . .

Taking into account the time effectively required to transmit the cease-fire order down to the lowest echelons of the combatant forces on both sides, the two parties are agreed that the cease-fire shall take effect completely and simultaneously for the different sectors of the country as follows:

Northern Vietnam at 8:00 A.M. (local time) on 27 July 1954

Central Vietnam at 8:00 A.M. (local time) on 1 August 1954

Southern Vietnam at 8:00 A.M. (local time) on 11 August 1954

It is agreed that Pekin mean time shall be taken as local time.

From such time as the cease-fire becomes effective in Northern Vietnam, both parties undertake not to engage in any large-scale offensive action in any part of the Indochinese theater of operations and not to commit the air forces based on Northern Vietnam outside that sector. The two parties also undertake to inform each other of their plans for movement from one regrouping zone to another within twenty-five (25) days of the present Agreement's entry into force.

12. All the operations and movements entailed in the cessation of hostilities and regrouping must proceed in a safe and orderly fashion:

(a) Within a certain number of days after the cease-fire Agreement shall have become effective, the number to be determined on the spot by the Trung Gia Military Commission, each party shall be responsible for removing and neutralizing mines (including river- and sea-mines), booby traps, explosives and any other dangerous substances placed by it. In the event of its being impossible to complete the work of removal and neutralization in time, the party concerned shall mark the spot by placing visible signs there. All demolitions, mine fields, wire entanglements and other hazards to the free movement of the personnel of the Joint Commission and its joint groups, known to be present after the withdrawal of the military forces, shall be reported to the Joint Commission by the Commanders of the opposing forces;

(b) From the time of the cease-fire until regrouping is completed on either side of the demarcation line:

(1) The forces of either party shall be provisionally

withdrawn from the provisional assembly areas assigned to the other party.

(2) When one party's forces withdraw by a route (road, rail, waterway, sea route) which passes through the territory of the other party (see Article 24), the latter party's forces must provisionally withdraw three kilometers on each side of such route, but in such a manner as to avoid interfering with the movements of the civil population.

13. From the time of the cease-fire until the completion of the movements from one regrouping zone into the other, civil and military transport aircraft shall follow air corridors between the provisional assembly areas assigned to the French Union forces north of the demarcation line on the one hand and the Loatian frontier and the regrouping zone assigned to the French Union forces on the other hand.

The position of the aircorridors, their width, the safety route for single-engined military aircraft transferred to the south and the search and rescue procedure for aircraft in distress shall be determined on the spot by the Trung Gia Military Commission.

14. Political and administrative measures in the two regrouping zones, on either side of the provisional military demarcation line:

(a) Pending the general elections which will bring about the unification of Vietnam, the conduct of civil administration in each regrouping zone shall be in the hands of the party whose forces are to be regrouped there in virtue of the present Agreement;

(b) Any territory controlled by one party which is transferred to the other party by the regrouping plan shall continue to be administered by the former party until such date as all the troops who are to be transferred have completely left that territory so as to free the zone assigned to the party in question. From then on, such territory shall be regarded as transferred to the other party, who shall assume responsibility for it.

Steps shall be taken to ensure that there is no break in the transfer of responsibilities. For this purpose, adequate notice shall be given by the withdrawing party to the other party, which shall make the necessary arrangements, in particular by sending administrative and police detachments to prepare for the assumption of administrative responsibility. The length of such notice shall be determined by the Trung Gia Military Commission. The transfer shall be effected in successive stages for the various territorial sectors.

The transfer of the civil administration of Hanoi and Haiphong to the authorities of the Democratic Republic of Vietnam shall be completed within the respective time limits laid down in Article 15 for military movements.

(c) Each party undertakes to refrain from any reprisals or discrimination against persons or organizations on account of their activities during the hostilities and to guarantee their democratic liberties.

(d) From the date of entry into force of the present Agreement until the movement of troops is completed,

any civilians residing in a district controlled by one
party who wish to go and live in the zone assigned
to the other party shall be permitted and helped to
do so by the authorities in that district.

15. The disengagement of the combatants, and the
withdrawals and transfers of military forces, equipment
and supplies shall take place in accordance with the following principles:

(a) The withdrawals and transfers of the military
forces, equipment and supplies of the two parties shall
be completed within three hundred (300) days, as laid
down in Article 2 of the present Agreement;

(b) Within either territory successive withdrawals
shall be made by sectors, portions of sectors or prov-
inces. Transfers from one regrouping zone to another
shall be made in successive monthly installments pro-
portionate to the number of troops to be transferred;

(c) The two parties shall undertake to carry out all
troop withdrawals and transfers in accordance with the
aims of the present Agreement, shall permit no hostile
act and shall take no step whatsoever which might
hamper such withdrawals and transfers. They shall
assist one another as far as this is possible;

(d) The two parties shall permit no destruction or
sabotage of any public property and no injury to the
life and property of the civil population. They shall
permit no interference in local civil administration;

(e) The Joint Commission and the International
Commission shall ensure that steps are taken to safe-
guard the forces in the course of withdrawal and transfer;

(f) The Trung Gia Military Commission, and later the Joint Commission, shall determine by common agreement the exact procedure for the disengagement of the combatants and for troop withdrawals and transfers, on the basis of the principles mentioned above and within the framework laid down below:

1. The disengagement of the combatants, including the concentration of the armed forces of all kinds and also each party's movements into the provisional assembly areas assigned to it and the other party's provisional withdrawal from it, shall be completed within a period not exceeding fifteen (15) days after the date when the cease-fire becomes effective.

The general delineation of the provisional assembly areas is set out in the maps not reprinted here annexed to the present Agreement.

In order to avoid any incidents, no troops shall be stationed less than 1,500 meters from the lines delimiting the provisional assembly areas.

During the period until the transfers are concluded, all the coastal islands west of the following lines shall be included in the Haiphong perimeter:

meridian of the southern point of Kebao Island

northern coast of the Ile Rouse (excluding the island), extended as far as the meridian of Champha-Mines

2. The withdrawals and transfers shall be effected in the following order and within the following periods (from the date of the entry into force of the present Agreement):

FORCES OF THE FRENCH UNION

	Days
Hanoi perimeter	80
Haiduong perimeter	100
Haiphong perimeter	300

FORCES OF THE PEOPLE'S ARMY OF VIETNAM

	Days
Ham Tan and Xuyenmec provisional assembly area	80
Central Vietnam provisional assembly area—first installment	80
Plain des Jons provisional assembly area . . .	100
Point Camau provisional assembly area . . .	200
Central Vietnam provisional assembly area—last installment	300

Chapter III. Ban on Introduction of Fresh Troops, Military Personnel, Arms and Munitions, Military Bases

16. With effect from the date of entry into force of the present Agreement, the introduction into Vietnam of any troop reinforcements and additional military personnel is prohibited.

It is understood, however, that the rotation of units and groups of personnel, the arrival in Vietnam of individual personnel on a temporary duty basis and the return to Vietnam of individual personnel after short periods of leave or temporary duty outside Vietnam shall be permitted under the conditions laid down below:

(a) Rotation of units (defined in paragraph (c) of this Article) and groups of personnel shall not be permitted for French Union troops stationed north of the provisional military demarcation line laid down in Article 1 of the present Agreement, during the withdrawal period provided for in Article 2.

However, under the heading of individual personnel not more than fifty (50) men, including officers, shall during any one month be permitted to enter that part of the country north of the provisional military demarcation line on a temporary duty basis or to return there after short periods of leave or temporary duty outside Vietnam.

(b) "Rotation" is defined as the replacement of units or groups of personnel by other units of the same echelon, or by personnel who are arriving in Vietnam territory to do their overseas service there;

(c) The units rotated shall never be larger than a battalion—or the corresponding echelon for air and naval forces;

(d) Rotation shall be conducted on a man-for-man basis, provided, however, that in any one quarter neither party shall introduce more than fifteen thousand five hundred (15,500) members of its armed forces into Vietnam under the rotation policy.

(e) Rotation units (defined in paragraph (c) of this Article) and groups of personnel, and the individual personnel mentioned in this Article, shall enter and leave Vietnam only through the entry points enumerated in Article 20 below:

(f) Each party shall notify the Joint Commission and the International Commission at least two days in advance of any arrivals or departures of units, groups of personnel and individual personnel in or from Vietnam. Reports on the arrivals or departures of units, groups of personnel and individual personnel in or from Vietnam shall be submitted daily to the Joint Commission and the International Commission.

All the above-mentioned notifications and reports shall indicate the places and dates of arrival or departure and the number of persons arriving or departing.

(g) The International Commission, through its Inspection Teams, shall supervise and inspect the rotation of units and groups of personnel and the arrival and departure of individual personnel as authorized above at the points of entry enumerated in Article 20 below.

17. (a) With effect from the date of entry into force of the present Agreement, the introduction into Vietnam of any reinforcements in the form of all types of arms, munitions and other war material, such as combat aircraft, naval craft, pieces of ordnance, jet engines and jet weapons, and armored vehicles, is prohibited.

(b) It is understood, however, that war material, arms, and munitions which have been destroyed, damaged, worn out, or used up after the cessation of hostilities may be replaced on the basis of piece-for-piece of the same type and with similar characteristics. Such replacements of war material, arms, and munitions shall not be permitted for French Union troops stationed north of the provisional military demarcation line laid down in Article 1 of the present Agreement, during the withdrawal period provided for in Article 2.

Naval craft may perform transport operations between the regrouping zones.

(c) The war material, arms, and munitions for replacement purposes, provided for in paragraph (b) of this Article, shall be introduced into Vietnam only through the points of entry enumerated in Article 20 below. War material, arms, and munitions to be replaced shall be shipped from Vietnam only through the points of entry enumerated in Article 20 below.

(d) Apart from the replacements permitted within the limits laid down in paragraph (b) of this Article, the introduction of war material, arms, and munitions of all types in the form of unassembled parts for subsequent assembly is prohibited.

(e) Each party shall notify the Joint Commission and the International Commission at least two days in advance of any arrivals or departures which may take place of war material, arms, and munitions of all types. In order to justify the requests for the introduction into Vietnam of arms, munitions, and other war material (as defined in paragraph (a) of this Article) for replacement purposes, a report concerning each incoming shipment shall be submitted to the Joint Commission and the International Commission. Such reports shall indicate the use made of the items so replaced.

(f) The International Commission, through its Inspection Teams, shall supervise and inspect the replacements permitted in the circumstances laid down in this Article.

18. With effect from the date of entry into force of

the present Agreement, the establishment of new military bases is prohibited throughout Vietnam territory.

19. With effect from the date of entry into force of the present Agreement, no military base under the control of a foreign State may be established in the regrouping zone of either party; the two parties shall ensure that the zones assigned to them do not adhere to any military alliance and are not used for the resumption of hostilities or to further an aggressive policy.

20. The points of entry into Vietnam for rotation personnel and replacements of material are fixed as follows:

—Zones to the north of the provisional military demarcation line: Laoky, Langson, Tien-Yen, Haiphong, Vinh, Dong-Hoi, Muong-Sen;

—Zones to the south of the provisional military demarcation line: Tourane, Quinhon, Nhatrang, Bangoi, Saigon, Cap St. Jacques, Tanchau.

Chapter IV. Prisoners of War and Civilian Internees

21. The liberation and repatriation of all prisoners of war and civilian internees detained by each of the two parties at the coming into force of the present Agreement shall be carried out under the following conditions:

(a) All prisoners of war and civilian internees of Vietnam, French, and other nationalities captured since the beginning of hostilities in Vietnam during military operations or in any other circumstances of war and in any part of the territory of Vietnam shall be liberated within a period of thirty (30) days after the date when the cease-fire becomes effective in each theater.

(b) The term "civilian internees" is understood to mean all persons who, having in any way contributed to the political and armed struggle between the two parties, have been arrested for that reason and have been kept in detention by either party during the period of hostilities.

(c) All prisoners of war and civilian internees held by either party shall be surrendered to the appropriate authorities of the other party, who shall give them all possible assistance in proceeding to their country of origin, place of habitual residence, or the zone of their choice.

Chapter V. Miscellaneous

22. The Commanders of the Forces of the two parties shall ensure that persons under their respective commands who violate any of the provisions of the present Agreement are suitably punished.

23. In cases in which the place of burial is known and the existence of graves has been established, the Commander of the Forces of either party shall, within a specific period after the entry into force of the Armistice Agreement, permit the graves service personnel of the other party to enter the part of Vietnam territory under their military control for the purpose of finding and removing the bodies of deceased military personnel

of that party, including the bodies of deceased prisoners of war. The Joint Commission shall determine the procedures and the time limit for the performance of this task. The Commanders of the Forces of the two parties shall communicate to each other all information in their possession as to the place of burial of military personnel of the other party.

24. The present Agreement shall apply to all the armed forces of either party. The armed forces of each party shall respect the demilitarized zone and the territory under the military control of the other party, and shall commit no act and undertake no operation against the other party and shall not engage in blockade of any kind in Vietnam.

For the purposes of the present Article, the word "territory" includes territorial waters and air space.

25. The Commanders of the Forces of the two parties shall afford full protection and all possible assistance and co-operation to the Joint Commission and its joint groups and to the International Commission and its inspection teams in the performance of the functions and tasks assigned to them by the present Agreement.

26. The costs involved in the operations of the Joint Commission and joint groups and of the International Commission and its Inspection Teams shall be shared equally between the two parties.

27. The signatories of the present Agreement and their successors in their functions shall be responsible for

ensuring and observance and enforcement of the terms and provisions thereof. The Commanders of the Forces of the two parties shall, within their respective commands, take all steps and make all arrangements necessary to ensure full compliance with all the provisions of the present Agreement by all elements and military personnel under their command.

The procedures laid down in the present Agreement shall, whenever necessary, be studied by the Commanders of the two parties and, if necessary, defined more specifically by the Joint Commission.

Chapter VI. Joint Commission and International Commission for Supervision and Control in Vietnam

28. Responsibility for the execution of the agreement on the cessation of hostilities shall rest with the parties.

29. An International Commission shall ensure the control and supervision of this execution.

30. In order to facilitate, under the conditions shown below, the execution of provisions concerning joint actions by the two parties, a Joint Commission shall be set up in Vietnam.

31. The Joint Commission shall be composed of an equal number of representatives of the Commanders of the two parties.

32. The Presidents of the delegations to the Joint Commission shall hold the rank of General.

The Joint Commission shall set up joint groups the number of which shall be determined by mutual agreement between the parties. The joint groups shall be composed of an equal number of officers from both parties. Their location on the demarcation line between the regrouping zones shall be determined by the parties whilst taking into account the powers of the Joint Commission.

33. The Joint Commission shall ensure the execution of the following provisions of the Agreement on the cessation of hostilities:

(a) A simultaneous and general cease-fire in Vietnam for all regular and irregular armed forces of the two parties.

(b) A regroupment of the armed forces of the two parties.

(c) Observance of the demarcation lines between the regrouping zones and of the demilitarized sectors.

Within the limits of its competence it shall help the parties to execute the said provisions, shall ensure liaison between them for the purpose of preparing and carrying out plans for the application of these provisions, and shall endeavor to solve such disputed questions as may arise between the parties in the course of executing these provisions.

34. An International Commission shall be set up for the control and supervision over the application of the provisions of the agreement on the cessation of hostilities in Vietnam. It shall be composed of representatives of the following States: Canada, India and Poland.

It shall be presided over by the Representative of India.

35. The International Commission shall set up fixed

and mobile Inspection Teams, composed of an equal number of officers appointed by each of the above-mentioned States. The fixed teams shall be located at the following points: Laoky, Langson, Tien-Yen, Haiphong, Vinh, Dong-Hoi, Muong-Sen, Tourane, Quinhon, Nhatrang, Bangoi, Saigon, Cap St. Jacques, Tanchau. These points of location may, at a later date, be altered at the request of the Joint Commission, or of one of the parties, or of the International Commission itself, by agreement between the International Commission and the command of the party concerned. The zones of action of the Mobile Teams shall be the regions bordering the land and sea frontiers of Vietnam, the demarcation lines between the regrouping zones and the demilitarized zones. Within the limits of these zones they shall have the right to move freely and shall receive from the local civil and military authorities all facilities they may require for the fulfillment of their tasks (provision of personnel, placing at their disposal documents needed for supervision, summoning witnesses necessary for holding inquiries, ensuring the security and freedom of movement of the Inspection Teams, etc.) . . . They shall have at their disposal such modern means of transport, observation, and communication as they may require. Beyond the zones of action as defined above, the Mobile Teams may, by agreement with the command of the party concerned, carry out other movements within the limits of the tasks given them by the present Agreement.

36. The International Commission shall be responsi-

ble for supervising the proper execution by the parties of the provisions of the agreement. For this purpose it shall fulfill the tasks of control, observation, inspection, and investigation connected with the application of the provisions of the agreement on the cessation of hostilities, and it shall in particular:

(a) Control the movement of the armed forces of the two parties, effected within the framework of the regroupment plan.

(b) Supervise the demarcation lines between the regrouping areas, and also demilitarized zones.

(c) Control the operations of releasing prisoners of war and civilian internees.

(d) Supervise at ports and airfields as well as along all frontiers of Vietnam the execution of the provisions of the agreement on the cessation of hostilities, regulating the introduction into the country of armed forces, military personnel and of all kinds of arms, munitions, and war material.

37. The International Commission shall, through the medium of the inspection teams mentioned above, and as soon as possible either on its own initiative or at the request of the Joint Commission, or of one of the parties, undertake the necessary investigations both documentary and on the ground.

38. The inspection teams shall submit to the International Commission the results of their supervision, their investigation and their observations, furthermore they shall draw up such special reports as they may consider necessary or as may be requested from them by the Commission. In the case of a disagreement

within the teams, the conclusions of each member shall be submitted to the Commission.

39. If any one inspection team is unable to settle an incident or considers that there is a violation or a threat of a serious violation the International Commission shall be informed; the latter shall study the reports and the conclusions of the inspection teams and shall inform the parties of the measures which should be taken for the settlement of the incident, ending of the violation or removal of the threat of violation.

40. When the Joint Commission is unable to reach an agreement on the interpretation to be given to some provision or on the appraisal of a fact, the International Commission shall be informed of the disputed question. Its recommendations shall be sent directly to the parties and shall be notified to the Joint Commission.

41. The recommendations of the International Commission shall be adopted by majority vote, subject to the provisions contained in Article 42. If the votes are divided the chairman's vote shall be decisive.

The International Commission may formulate recommendations concerning amendments and additions which should be made to the provisions of the agreement on the cessation of hostilities in Vietnam, in order to ensure a more effective execution of that agreement. These recommendations shall be adopted unanimously.

42. When dealing with questions concerning violations, or threats of violations, which might lead to a resumption of hostilities, namely:

(a) Refusal by the armed forces of one party to effect the movements provided for in the regroupment plan;

(b) Violation by the armed forces of one of the parties of the regrouping zones, territorial waters, or air space of the other party;

the decisions of the International Commission must be unanimous.

43. If one of the parties refuses to put into effect a recommendation of the International Commission, the parties concerned or the Commission itself shall inform the members of the Geneva Conference.

If the International Commission does not reach unanimity in the cases provided for in Article 42, it shall submit a majority report and one or more minority reports to the members of the Conference.

The International Commission shall inform the members of the Conference in all cases where its activity is being hindered.

44. The International Commission shall be set up at the time of the cessation of hostilities in Indochina in order that it should be able to fulfill the tasks provided for in Article 36.

45. The International Commission for Supervision and Control in Vietnam shall act in close co-operation with the International Commissions for Supervision and Control in Cambodia and Laos.

The Secretaries-General of these three Commissions shall be responsible for co-ordinating their work and for relations between them.

46. The International Commission for Supervision and Control in Vietnam may, after consultation with

the International Commissions for Supervision and Control in Cambodia and Laos, and having regard to the development of the situation in Cambodia and Laos, progressively reduce its activities. Such a decision must be adopted unanimously.

47. All the provisions of the present Agreement, save the second sub-paragraph of Article 11, shall enter into force at 2400 hours (Geneva time) on 22 July 1954.

Done in Geneva at 2400 hours on the 20th of July 1954 in French and in Vietnamese, both texts being equally authenic.

For the Commander-in-Chief of
the People's Army of Vietnam
Ta-Quang Buu,
Vice-Minister of National Defense
of the Democratic Republic
of Vietnam

For the Commander-in-Chief of
the French Union Forces in
Indo-China
Brigadier-General Delteil.

FINAL DECLARATION OF THE GENEVA CONFERENCE (*July 21, 1954*)

1. The Conference takes note of the agreements ending hostilities in Cambodia, Laos, and Vietnam and organizing international control and the super-

vision of the execution of the provisions of these agreements.

2. The Conference expresses satisfaction at the ending of hostilities in Cambodia, Laos, and Vietnam; the Conference expresses its conviction that the execution of the provisions set out in the present declaration and in the agreements on the cessation of hostilities will permit Cambodia, Laos, and Vietnam henceforth to play their part, in full independence and sovereignty, in the peaceful community of nations.

3. The Conference takes note of the declarations made by the governments of Cambodia and of Laos of their intention to adopt measures permitting all citizens to take their place in the national community, in particular by participating in the next general elections, which, in conformity with the constitution of each of these countries, shall take place in the course of the year 1955, by secret ballot and in conditions of respect for fundamental freedoms.

4. The Conference takes note of the clauses in the agreement on the cessation of hostilities in Vietnam prohibiting the introduction into Vietnam of foreign troops and military personnel as well as of all kinds of arms and munitions. The Conference also takes note of the declarations made by the Governments of Cambodia and Laos of their resolution not to request foreign aid, whether in war material, in personnel, or in instructors except for the purpose of the effective defense of their territory and, in the case of Laos, to the extent defined by the agreements on the cessation of hostilities in Laos.

5. The Conference takes note of the clauses in the

agreement on the cessation of hostilities in Vietnam to the effect that no military base under the control of a foreign State may be established in the regrouping zones of the two parties, the latter having the obligation to see that the zones allotted to them shall not constitute part of any military alliance and shall not be utilized for the resumption of hostilities or in the service of an aggressive policy. The Conference also takes note of the declarations of the Governments of Cambodia and Laos to the effect that they will not join in any agreement with other States if this agreement includes the obligation to participate in a military alliance not in conformity with the principles of the Charter of the United Nations or, in the case of Laos, with the principles of the agreement on the cessation of hostilities in Laos or, so long as their security is not threatened, the obligation to establish bases on Cambodian or Laotian territory for the military forces of foreign powers.

6. The Conference recognizes that the essential purpose of the agreement relating to Vietnam is to settle military questions with a view to ending hostilities and that the military demarcation line is provisional and should not in any way be interpreted as constituting a political or territorial boundary. The Conference expresses its conviction that the execution of the provisions set out in the present declaration and in the agreement on the cessation of hostilities creates the necessary basis for the achievement in the near future of a political settlement in Vietnam.

7. The Conference declares that, so far as Vietnam is concerned, the settlement of political problems,

effected on the basis of respect for the principles of independence, unity, and territorial integrity, shall permit the Vietnamese people to enjoy the fundamental freedoms, guaranteed by democratic institutions established as a result of free general elections by secret ballot. In order to ensure that sufficient progress in the restoration of peace has been made, and that all the necessary conditions obtain for free expression of the national will, general elections shall be held in July, 1956, under the supervision of an international commission composed of representatives of the Member States of the International Supervisory Commission, referred to in the agreement on the cessation of hostilities. Consultations will be held on this subject between the competent representative authorities of the two zones from July 20, 1955, onward.

8. The provisions of the agreements on the cessation of hostilities intended to ensure the protection of individuals and of property must be most strictly applied and must, in particular, allow everyone in Vietnam to decide freely in which zone he wishes to live.

9. The competent representative authorities of the North and South zones of Vietnam, as well as the authorities of Laos and Cambodia, must not permit any individual or collective reprisals against persons who have collaborated in any way with one of the parties during the war, or against members of such persons' families.

10. The Conference takes note of the declaration of the Government of the French Republic to the effect that it is ready to withdraw its troops from the territory of Cambodia, Laos, and Vietnam, at the

94

request of the governments concerned and within periods which shall be fixed by agreement between the parties except in the cases where, by agreement between the two parties, a certain number of French troops shall remain at specified points and for a specified time.

11. The Conference takes note of the declaration of the French Government to the effect that for the settlement of all the problems connected with the reestablishment and consolidation of peace in Cambodia, Laos, and Vietnam, the French Government will proceed from the principle of respect for the independence and sovereignty, unity, and territorial integrity of Cambodia, Laos, and Vietnam.

12. In their relations with Cambodia, Laos, and Vietnam, each member of the Geneva Conference undertakes to respect the sovereignty, the independence, the unity, and the territorial integrity of the above-mentioned States, and to refrain from any interference in their internal affairs.

13. The members of the Conference agree to consult one another on any question which may be referred to them by the International Supervisory Commission, in order to study such measures as may prove necessary to ensure that the agreements on the cessation of hostilities in Cambodia, Laos, and Vietnam are respected.

THE UNITED STATES POSITION

Unilateral Declaration Presented at the Close of the Geneva Conference by Mr. Bedell Smith (July 21, 1954)

The Government of the United States being resolved to devote its efforts to the strengthening of peace in accordance with the principles and purposes of the United Nations

Takes Note of the Agreements concluded at Geneva on July 20 and 21, 1954, between (a) the Franco-Laotian Command and the Command of the People's Army of Vietnam; (b) the Royal Khmer Army Command and the Command of the People's Army of Vietnam; (c) the Franco-Vietnamese Command and the Command of the People's Army of Vietnam, and of paragraphs 1 to 12 of the Declaration presented to the Geneva Conference on July 21, 1954.

The Government of the United States of America

Declares with regard to the aforesaid Agreements and paragraphs that (i) it will refrain from the threat or the use of force to disturb them, in accordance with Article 2 (Section 4) of the Charter of the United Nations dealing with the obligation of Members to refrain in their international relations from the threat or use of force; and (ii) it would view any renewal of the aggression in violation of the aforesaid Agreements with grave concern and as seriously threatening international peace and security.

In connection with the statement in the Declaration

concerning free elections in Vietnam, my government wishes to make clear its position which it has expressed in a Declaration made in Washington on June 29, 1954, as follows:

"In the case of nations now divided against their will, we shall continue to seek to achieve unity through free elections, supervised by the United Nations to ensure that they are conducted fairly."

With respect to the statement made by the Representative of the State of Vietnam, the United States reiterates its traditional position that peoples are entitled to determine their own future and that it will not join in an arrangement which would hinder this. Nothing in its declaration just made is intended to or does indicate any departure from this traditional position.

We share the hope that the agreement will permit Cambodia, Laos, and Vietnam to play their part in full independence and sovereignty, in the peaceful community of nations, and will enable the peoples of that area to determine their own future. . . .

Fourteen Points for Peace in Southeast Asia

[*Secretary of State Dean Rusk's Fourteen Points are the fullest statement of our terms for settlement in Vietnam, although their general nature leaves many questions unanswered. They should be compared with the terms set forth by the communists in the documents that follow.*]

The following statements are on the public record about elements which the U.S. believes can go into peace in Southeast Asia:

1. The Geneva Agreements of 1954 and 1962 are an adequate basis for peace in Southeast Asia;

2. We would welcome a conference on Southeast Asia or on any part thereof;

3. We would welcome "negotiations without preconditions" as the seventeen nations put it;

4. We would welcome unconditional discussions as President Johnson put it;

5. A cessation of hostilities could be the first order of business at a conference or could be the subject of preliminary discussions;

6. Hanoi's four points could be discussed along with other points which others might wish to propose;

7. We want no U.S. bases in Southeast Asia;

8. We do not desire to retain U.S. troops in South Vietnam after peace is assured;

9. We support free elections in South Vietnam to give the South Vietnamese a government of their own choice;

10. The question of reunification of Vietnam should be determined by the Vietnamese through their own free decision;

11. The countries of Southeast Asia can be non-aligned or neutral if that be their option;

12. We would much prefer to use our resources for the economic reconstruction of Southeast Asia than in war. If there is peace, North Vietnam could participate in a regional effort to which we would be prepared to contribute at least one billion dollars;

13. The President has said "The Viet Cong would not have difficulty being represented and having their views represented if for a moment Hanoi decided she wanted to cease aggression. I don't think that would be an insurmountable problem."

14. We have said publicly and privately that we could stop the bombing of North Vietnam as a step toward peace although there has not been the slightest hint or suggestion from the other side as to what they would do if the bombing stopped.

Hanoi's Four Points

[*North Vietnam's Four Points were set forth in a speech by Premier Pham Van Dong on April 8, 1965. It is important to note that they are presented as an interpretation of the Geneva Agreements, which both sides say would be a fair basis for settlement. The basic point of dispute revolves around Point 3, which incorporates by reference the Program of the National Liberation Front.*]

The unswerving policy of the DRV government is to respect strictly the 1954 Geneva Agreements on Vietnam and to implement correctly their basic provisions as embodied in the following points:

1. Recognition of the basic national rights of the Vietnamese people—peace, independence, sovereignty, unity, and territorial integrity. According to the Geneva Agreements, the U.S. government must withdraw from South Vietnam U.S. troops, military personnel, and weapons of all kinds, dismantle all U.S. military bases there, and cancel its military alliance with South Vietnam. It must end its policy of intervention and aggression in South Vietnam. According to the Geneva Agreements, the U.S. government must stop its acts of war

against North Vietnam and completely cease all encroachments on the territory and sovereignty of the DRV.

2. Pending the peaceful reunification of Vietnam, while Vietnam is still temporarily divided into two zones, the military provisions of the 1954 Geneva Agreements on Vietnam must be strictly respected. The two zones must refrain from entering into any military alliance with foreign countries and there must be no foreign military bases, troops, or military personnel in their respective territory.

3. The internal affairs of South Vietnam must be settled by the South Vietnamese people themselves in accordance with the program of the NFLSV, without any foreign interference.

4. The peaceful reunification of Vietnam is to be settled by the Vietnamese people in both zones, without any foreign interference.

This stand of the DRV government unquestionably enjoys the approval and support of all peace- and justice-loving governments and peoples in the world. The government of the DRV is of the view that the stand expounded here is the basis for the soundest political settlement of the Vietnam problem.

If this basis is recognized, favorable conditions will be created for the peaceful settlement of the Vietnam question, and it will be possible to consider the reconvening of an international conference along the pattern of the 1954 Geneva Conference on Vietnam.

The DRV government declares that any approach contrary to the aforementioned stand is inappropriate;

any approach tending to secure U.N. intervention in the Vietnam situation is also inappropriate. Such approaches are basically at variance with the 1954 Geneva Agreements on Vietnam.

We have indicated that the other three points are generally acceptable; in fact, they coincide pretty much with our own positions.

The Official Program of the NLF

[*The official Program of the National Liberation Front of South Vietnam as broadcast by Hanoi on February 11, 1961, is the substance of Point 3 of the famous Four Points, although its precise contents have varied from time to time.*]

1. To overthrow the disguised colonial regime of the U.S. imperialists and the dictatorial Ngo Dinh Diem administration, lackey of the United States, and to form a national democratic coalition administration.

The present regime in South Vietnam is a disguised colonial regime of the U.S. imperialists. The South Vietnamese administration is a lackey which has been carrying out the U.S. imperialists' political lines. This regime and administration must be overthrown, and a broad national democratic coalition administration formed to include representatives of all strata of the people, nationalities, political parties, religious communities, and patriotic personages; to wrest back the people's economic, political, social, and cultural interests; to realize independence and democracy; to improve the people's living conditions; and to carry out a policy of peace and neutrality and advance toward peaceful reunification of the fatherland.

2. To bring into being a broad and progressive democracy.

a. To abolish the current constitution of the Ngo Dinh Diem dictatorial administration, lackey of the United States, and to elect a new National Assembly through universal suffrage.

b. To promulgate all democratic freedoms: freedom of expression, of the press, of assembly, of association of movement . . . (ellipsis as received); to guarantee freedom of belief with no discrimination toward any religion on the part of the state; and to grant freedom of action to the patriotic political parties and mass organizations, irrespective of political tendencies.

c. To grant general amnesty to all political detainees, dissolve all concentration camps under any form whatsoever, abolish the fascist law 10-59 and other antidemocratic laws; and to grant the right of repatriation to all those who had to flee abroad due to the U.S.-Diem regime.

d. To strictly ban all illegal arrests and imprisonments and tortures, and to punish unrepenting cruel murderers of the people.

3. To build an independent and sovereign economy, and improve the people's living conditions.

a. To abolish the economic monopoly of the United States and its henchmen; to build an independent and sovereign economy and finance, beneficial to the nation and people; and to confiscate and nationalize the property of the U.S. imperialists and the ruling clique, their stooges.

b. To help the industrialists and trades people rehabilitate and develop industry both large and small, and to encourage industrial development; and to actively protect homemade products by abolishing production taxes, restricting or ending the import of those goods which can be produced in the country, and reducing taxes of import of raw materials and machinery.

c. To rehabilitate agriculture, and to modernize planting, fishing, and animal husbandry; to help peasants reclaim waste land and develop production; and to protect crops and insure the consumption of agricultural products.

d. To encourage and accelerate the economic interflow between the town and the countryside, between plains and mountainous areas; and to develop trade with foreign countries without distinction of political regimes and on the principle of equality and mutual benefits.

e. To apply an equitable and rational system to abolish arbitrary fines.

f. To promulgate labor regulations, that is: to prohibit dismissals, wage cuts, fines and ill treatment of workers; to improve the life of workers and office employees; and to fix wages and guarantees for the health of teen-age apprentices.

g. To organize social relief: jobs for unemployed; protection of orphans, elders, and the disabled; assistance to those who have become disabled or lost their relatives in the struggle against U.S. imperialism and its stooges; and relief to localities suffering crop failures, fire, and natural calamities.

h. To help northern compatriots who had been forced or enticed by the reactionaries to go south after the restoration of peace to return to their native places if they so desire, and to provide jobs to those who decide to remain in the south.

i. To strictly prohibit forcible house removals, arson, usurpation of land, and the herding of the people into concentration centers; and to insure the country folk and urban working people of the opportunity to earn their living in security.

4. To carry out land rent reduction in preparation for the settlement of the agrarian problem so as to insure land to the tillers.

a. To carry out land rent reduction; to guarantee the peasants' right to till their present plots of land and insure the right of ownership for those who have reclaimed waste land; and to protect the legitimate right of ownership by peasants of the plots of land distributed to them during the resistance war.

b. To abolish the "prosperity zones" and the policy of herding the people into "resettlement centers" and to grant the right of those forcibly herded into "prosperity zones" or "resettlement centers" (disguised concentration camps) (parentheses as received) to return home freely and earn their living on their own plots of land.

c. To confiscate the land usurped by the U.S. imperialists and their agents and distribute it to landless and land-poor peasants; and to redistribute communal land in an equitable and rational way.

d. Through negotiations, the state will purchase from landowners at equitable and rational prices all land held by them in excess of a given area, fixed in accordance with the concrete situation in each locality, and distribute it to landless and land-poor peasants.

This land will be distributed free and will be free of any conditions.

5. To build a national and democratic education and culture.

a. To eliminate the enslaving and gangster-style American culture and education; and to build a rational, progressive culture and education serving the fatherland and the people.

b. To wipe out illiteracy; to build sufficient general education schools for the youth and children; to expand universities and professional schools; to use the Vietnamese language in teaching; to reduce school fees or exempt fees for poor pupils and students; and to reform the examination system.

c. To develop science and technology and the national literature and art; and to encourage and help intellectuals, cultural, and art workers to develop their abilities in service of national construction.

d. To develop medical service in order to look after the people's health; and to expand the gymnastic and sports movement.

6. To build an army to defend the motherland and the people.

a. To build a national army defending the fatherland and the people; and to cancel the system of U.S. military advisers.

b. To abolish the pressganging regime; to improve the material life of the armymen and insure their political rights; to prohibit the ill-treatment of soldiers; and to apply a policy of assistance to families of poor armymen.

c. To remunerate and give worthy jobs to those officers and soldiers who have rendered meritorious services in the struggle against the domination of the U.S. imperialists and their henchmen; and to observe leniency toward those who had before collaborated with the U.S.-Diem clique and committed crimes against the people, but have now repented and serve the people.

d. To abolish all the military bases of foreign countries in South Vietnam.

7. To guarantee the right of equality between nationalities and between men and women; to protect the legitimate rights of foreign residents and overseas Vietnamese.

a. To insure the right of autonomy of the national minorities; to set up, within the framework of the great family of the Vietnamese people, autonomous regions, areas inhabited by minority peoples; to insure equal rights among different nationalities, allowing all nationalities to have the right to use and develop their own spoken and written languages and to preserve or change their customs and habits; to abolish the U.S.-Diem clique's present policy of ill-treatment and forced assimilation of the minority nationalities; and to help the minority peoples to catch up with the common level of the people by developing the economy and culture in the areas inhabited by them, by training skilled personnel from people of minority origin.

b. To insure the right of equality between men and women, so women can enjoy the same rights as men in all fields: political, economic, cultural, and social.

c. To protect the legitimate rights of foreigners residing in Vietnam; and to defend and care for Vietnamese nationals abroad.

8. To carry out a foreign policy of peace and neutrality.

a. To cancel all unequal treaties signed with foreign countries by the U.S. henchmen which violate national sovereignty.

b. To establish diplomatic relations with all countries irrespective of political regime, in accordance with the principles of peaceful coexistence as put forth at the Bandung conference.

c. To unite closely with the peace-loving and neutral countries; and to expand friendly relations with Asian and African countries, first of all, with neighboring Cambodia and Laos.

d. To refrain from joining any bloc or military alliance or forming a military alliance with any country.

e. To receive economic aid from any country ready to assist Vietnam without conditions attached.

9. To establish normal relations between North and South Vietnam as a first step toward peaceful reunification of the country.

The urgent demand of our people throughout the country is to reunify the country by peaceful means. The NFLSV undertakes the gradual reunification of the country by peaceful means, on the principle of negotiations and discussions between the two zones of all forms and measures beneficial to the people and fatherland. Pending the national reunification, the governments of the two zones will negotiate and undertake not to spread propaganda to divide the peoples or favor war, nor to use military forces against each other; to carry out economic and cultural exchanges between the two zones; and to insure for people of both zones freedom of movement, of livelihood, and the right of mutual visits and correspondence.

10. To oppose aggressive war and actively defend world peace.

a. To oppose aggressive wars and all forms of enslavement by the imperialists; and to support the national liberation struggles of peoples in various countries.

b. To oppose war propaganda; and to demand general disarmament, prohibition of nuclear weapons, and demand the use of atomic energy for peaceful purposes.

c. To support the movements for peace, democracy, and social progress in the world; and to actively contribute to the safeguarding of peace in Southeast Asia and the world.

The SEATO Treaty

[*Article IV is the basis for the claim of an American Treaty commitment. It was originally assumed that section 2 of that article was applicable to the war in Vietnam. That section deals with threat "other than by armed attack," and was designed specifically to deal with subversion and internal revolution. It merely commits the parties to consult on measures. Under the new interpretation the action of Hanoi is considered an "armed attack," thus bringing Section I of Article IV into operation. However, even if this premise is accepted, as I have previously explained at length, this article does not commit the United States to use combat forces in support of South Vietnam. The text of the SEATO Treaty was signed in September, 1954, and ratified in February, 1955. The signatories were Australia, France, New Zealand, Pakistan, the Philippines, the United Kingdom, and the United States.*]

SOUTHEAST ASIA COLLECTIVE DEFENSE TREATY

The Parties to this Treaty,

Recognizing the sovereign equality of all the Parties,

Reiterating their faith in the purposes and principles set forth in the Charter of the United Nations and their desire to live in peace with all peoples and all governments,

Reaffirming that, in accordance with the Charter of the United Nations, they uphold the principle of equal rights and self-determination of peoples, and declaring that they will earnestly strive by every peaceful means to promote self-government and to secure the independence of all countries whose people desire it and are able to undertake its responsibilities,

Desiring to strengthen the fabric of peace and freedom and to uphold the principles of democracy, individual liberty and the rule of law, and to promote the economic well-being and development of all peoples in the treaty area,

Intending to declare publicly and formally their sense of unity, so that any potential aggressor will appreciate that the Parties stand together in the area, and

Desiring further to coordinate their efforts for collective defense for the preservation of peace and security,

Therefore agree as follows:

Article I

The Parties undertake, as set forth in the Charter of the United Nations, to settle any international disputes in which they may be involved by peaceful means in such a manner that international peace and security and justice are not endangered, and to refrain in their international relations from the threat or use of force in any manner inconsistent with the purposes of the United Nations.

Article II

In order more effectively to achieve the objectives of this Treaty, the Parties, separately and jointly, by means of continuous and effective self-help and mutual aid will maintain and develop their individual and collective capacity to resist armed attack and to prevent and counter subversive activities directed from without against their territorial integrity and political stability.

Article III

The Parties undertake to strengthen their free institutions and to cooperate with one another in the further development of economic measures, including technical assistance, designed both to promote economic progress and social well-being and to further the individual and collective efforts of governments toward these ends.

Article IV

1. Each Party recognizes that aggression by means of armed attack in the treaty area against any of the Parties or against any State or territory which the Parties by unanimous agreement may hereafter designate, would endanger its own peace and safety, and agrees that it will in that event act to meet the common danger in accordance with its constitutional processes. Measures taken under this paragraph shall be immedi-

Triumph or Tragedy

ately reported to the Security Council of the United Nations.

2. If, in the opinion of any of the Parties, the inviolability or the integrity of the territory or the sovereignty or political independence of any Party in the treaty area or of any other State or territory to which the provisions of paragraph 1 of this Article from time to time apply is threatened in any way other than by armed attack or is affected or threatened by any fact or situation which might endanger the peace of the area, the Parties shall consult immediately in order to agree on the measures which should be taken for the common defense.

3. It is understood that no action on the territory of any State designated by unanimous agreement under paragraph 1 of this Article or on any territory so designated shall be taken except at the invitation or with the consent of the government concerned.

Article V

The Parties hereby establish a Council, on which each of them shall be represented, to consider matters concerning the implementation of this Treaty. The Council shall provide for consultation with regard to military and any other planning as the situation obtaining in the treaty area may from time to time require. The Council shall be so organized as to be able to meet at any time.

Article VI

This Treaty does not not affect and shall not be interpreted as affecting in any way the rights and obligations of any of the Parties under the Charter of the United Nations or the responsibility of the United Nations for the maintenance of international peace and security. Each Party declares that none of the international engagements now in force between it and any other of the Parties or any third party is in conflict with the provisions of this Treaty, and undertakes not to enter into any international engagement in conflict with this Treaty.

Article VII

Any other State in a position to further the objectives of this Treaty and to contribute to the security of the area may, by unanimous agreement of the Parties, be invited to accede to this Treaty. Any State so invited may become a Party to the Treaty by depositing its instrument of accession with the Government of the Republic of the Philippines. The Government of the Republic of the Philippines shall inform each of the Parties of the deposit of each such instrument of accession.

Article VIII

As used in this Treaty, the "treaty area" is the general area of Southeast Asia, including also the entire territories of the Asian Parties, and the general area of the Southwest Pacific not including the Pacific area north of 21 degrees 30 minutes north latitude. The Parties may, by unanimous agreement, amend this Ar-

ticle to include within the treaty area the territory of
any State acceding to this Treaty in accordance with
Article VII or otherwise to change the treaty area.

Article IX

1. This Treaty shall be deposited in the archives of
the Government of the Republic of the Philippines.
Duly certified copies thereof shall be transmitted by
that government to the other signatories.

2. The Treaty shall be ratified and its provisions carried out by the Parties in accordance with their respective constitutional processes. The instruments of ratification shall be deposited as soon as possible with the
Government of the Republic of the Philippines, which
shall notify all of the other signatories of such deposit.

3. The Treaty shall enter into force between the
States which have ratified it as soon as the instruments
of ratification of a majority of the signatories shall have
been deposited, and shall come into effect with respect
to each other State on the date of the deposit of its
instrument of ratification.

Article X

This Treaty shall remain in force indefinitely, but
any Party may cease to be a Party one year after its notice of denunciation has been given to the Government
of the Republic of the Philippines, which shall inform
the Governments of the other Parties of the deposit of
each notice of denunciation.

Article XI

The English text of this Treaty is binding on the Parties, but when the Parties have agreed to the French text thereof and have so notified the Government of the Republic of the Philippines, the French text shall be equally authentic and binding on the Parties.

Understanding of the United States of America

The United States of America in executing the present Treaty does so with the understanding that its recognition of the effect of aggression and armed attack and its agreement with reference thereto in Article IV, paragraph 1, apply only to communist aggression but affirms that in the event of other aggression or armed attack it will consult under the provisions of Article IV, paragraph 2. . . .

Done at Manila this eighth day of September, 1954.

President Johnson's Position

[The President's press conference statement of July 28, 1965, announcing a substantial increase in our combat troop strength in Vietnam. It is among the most complete Presidential statements of our policy.]

My fellow Americans. Not long ago, I received a letter from a woman in the Midwest. She wrote:

"Dear Mr. President,

"In my humble way I am writing to you about The crisis in Vietnam. I have a son who is now in Vietnam. My husband served in World War II. Our country was at war. But now, this time, it's just something that I don't understand. Why?"

Well, I've tried to answer that question dozens of times and more in practically every state in this Union. I have discussed it fully in Baltimore in April, in Washington in May, in San Francisco in June. And let me again now discuss it here in the East Room of the White House.

Why must young Americans, born into a land exultant with hope and with golden promise, toil and suffer and sometimes die in such a remote and distant place?

The answer, like the war itself, is not an easy one.

But it echoes clearly from the painful lessons of half a century.

Three times in my lifetime—in two world wars and in Korea—Americans have gone to far lands to fight for freedom. We have learned at a terrible and a brutal cost that retreat does not bring safety, and weakness does not bring peace.

And it is this lesson that has brought us to Vietnam.

This is a different kind of war. There are no marching armies or solemn declarations. Some citizens of South Vietnam, at times with understandable grievances, have joined in the attack on their own Government.

But we must not let this mask the central fact that this is really war. It is guided by North Vietnam and it is spurred by Communist China. Its goal is to conquer the South, to defeat American power and to extend the Asiatic dominion of Communism.

And there are great stakes in the balance.

Most of the non-Communist nations of Asia cannot, by themselves and alone, resist the growing might and the grasping ambition of Asian Communism.

Our power therefore is a very vital shield. If we are driven from the field in Vietnam, then no nation can ever again have the same confidence in American promise or in American protection.

In each land, the forces of independence would be considerably weakened, and an Asia so threatened by Communist domination would certainly imperil the security of the United States itself.

We did not choose to be the guardians at the gate, but there is no one else. Nor would surrender in Vietnam bring peace, because we learned from Hitler at Munich that success only feeds the appetite of aggression. The battle would be renewed in one country, and then another country, bringing with it perhaps even larger and crueler conflict, as we have learned from the lessons of history.

Moreover, we are in Vietnam to fulfill one of the most solemn pledges of the American nation. Three Presidents—President Eisenhower, President Kennedy and your present President—over eleven years have committed themselves and have promised to help defend this small and valiant nation.

Strengthened by that promise, the people of South Vietnam have fought for many long years. Thousands of them have died. Thousands more have been crippled and scarred by war. And we just cannot now dishonor our word, or abandon our commitment, or leave those who believed us and who trusted us to the terror and repression and murder that would follow.

This, then, my fellow Americans, is why we are in Vietnam.

What are our goals in that war-stained land?

First, we intend to convince the Communists that we cannot be defeated by force of arms or by superior power. They are not easily convinced. In recent months they have greatly increased their fighting forces and their attacks and the numbers of incidents.

I have asked the commanding general, General Westmoreland, what more he needs to meet this mounting aggression. He has told me. And we will meet his needs.

I have today ordered to Vietnam the Airmobile Division and certain other forces which will raise our fighting strength from 75,000 to 125,000 men almost immediately. Additional forces will be needed later and they will be sent as requested.

This will make it necessary to increase our active fighting forces by raising the monthly draft call from 17,000 over a period of time to 35,000 per month and for us to step up our campaign for voluntary enlistments.

After this past week of deliberations, I have concluded that it is not essential to order Reserve units into service now. If that necessity should later be indicated, I will give the matter most careful consideration and I will give the country due and adequate notice before taking such action, but only after full preparations.

We have also discussed with the Government of South Vietnam lately the steps that . . . we will take to substantially increase their own effort, both on the battlefield and toward reform and progress in the villages. Ambassador Lodge is now formulating a new program to be tested upon his return to that area.

I have directed Secretary Rusk and Secretary McNamara to be available immediately to the Congress to review with these committees—the appropriate Congressional committees—what we plan to do in these areas. I have asked them to be able to answer the questions of any member of Congress.

And Secretary McNamara, in addition, will ask the Senate Appropriations Committee to add a limited amount to present legislation to help meet part of this new cost until a supplemental measure is ready and hearings can be held when the Congress assembles in January. In the meantime, we will use the authority contained in the present defense appropriation bill under consideration to transfer funds in addition to the additional money that we will ask.

These steps, like our actions in the past, are carefully measured to do what must be done to bring an end to aggression and a peaceful settlement.

We do not want an expanding struggle with consequences that no one can foresee, nor will we bluster or bully or flaunt our power. But we will not surrender, and we will not retreat.

For behind our American pledge lies the determination and resources, I believe, of all of the American nation.

Second, once the Communists know, as we know, that a violent solution is impossible, then a peaceful solution is inevitable. We are ready now, as we have always been, to move from the battlefield to the conference table.

I have stated publicly and many times, again and again, America's willingness to begin unconditional discussions with any Government at any place at any time.

Fifteen efforts have been made to start these discussions, with the help of forty nations throughout the world. But there has been no answer. But we are going to continue to persist, if persist we must, until death and desolation have led to the same conference table where others could now join us at a much smaller cost.

I have spoken many times of our objectives in Vietnam. So has the Government of South Vietnam. Hanoi has set forth its own proposals. We are ready to discuss their proposals and our proposals and any proposals of any Government whose people may be affected, for we fear the meeting room no more than we fear the battlefield. And in this pursuit we welcome and we ask for the concern and the assistance of any nation and all nations.

And if the United Nations and its officials or any one of its 114 members can by deed or word, private initiative or public action, bring us nearer an honorable peace, then they will have the support and gratitude of the United States of America.

I've directed Ambassador Goldberg to go to New York today and to present immediately to Secretary General U Thant a letter from me requesting that all the resources and the energy and the immense prestige of the United Nations be employed to find ways to halt aggression and to bring peace in Vietnam.

I made a similar request at San Francisco a few weeks ago because we do not seek the destruction of any Government nor do we covet a foot of any territory. But we insist and we will always insist that the people of South Vietnam shall have the right of choice, the right to shape their own destiny in free elections in the South or throughout all Vietnam under international supervision, and they shall not have any Government imposed upon them by force and terror so long as we can prevent it.

This was the purpose of the 1954 agreements which the Communists have now cruelly shattered. And if the machinery of those agreements was tragically weak, its purposes still guide our action. And as battle rages we will continue as best we can to help the good people of South Vietnam enrich the condition of their life, to feed the hungry, and to tend the sick, and teach the young, and shelter the homeless and help the farmer to increase his crops and the worker to find a job.

It is an ancient but still terrible irony that while many leaders of men create division in pursuit of grand ambitions, the children of men are really united in the simple, elusive desire for a life of fruitful and rewarding toil.

As I said in Johns Hopkins at Baltimore, I hope that one day we can help all the people of Asia toward that desire—and Eugene Black has made great progress since my appearance at Baltimore in that direction—not as the price of peace, for we are ready always to bear a more painful cost, but rather as a part of our obligations of justice toward our fellow man.

And let me also add now a personal note. I do not find it easy to send the flower of our youth, our finest young men, into battle. I have spoken to you today of the divisions and the forces and the battalions and the units, but I know them all, every one. I have seen them in a thousand streets of a hundred towns in every state in this Union—working and laughing and building and filled with hope and life. And I think I know, too, how their mothers weep and how their families sorrow.

And this is the most agonizing and the most painful duty of your President.

And there is something else, too. When I was young, poverty was so common that we didn't know it had a name. An education was something that you had to fight for, and water was really life itself. I have now been in public life for thirty-five years, more than three decades, and in each of those thirty-five years I have seen good men and wise leaders struggle to bring the blessings of this land to all of our people.

And now I am the President. It is now my opportunity to help every child get an education, to help every Negro and every American citizen have an equal opportunity, to help every family get a decent home, and to help bring healing to the sick and dignity to the old.

As I have said before, that is what I've lived for, that's what I've wanted all my life since I was a little boy, and I do not want to see all those hopes and all those dreams of so many people for so many years now drowned in the wasteful ravages of cruel wars. And I'm going to do all I can do to see that that never happens.

But I also know, as a realistic public servant, that as long as there are men who hate and destroy we must have the courage to resist or we'll see it all—all that we have built, all that we hope to build, all of our dreams for freedom, all, all—will be swept away on the flood of conquest.

So, too, this shall not happen. We will stand in Vietnam. . . .

Q. Mr. President, you haven't talked about a timetable in connection with Vietnam. You have said and you repeated today that the United States will not be defeated, will not grow tired.

Donald Johnson, national commander of the American Legion, went over to Vietnam in the spring and later called on you. He told White House reporters that he could imagine the war over there going on for five, six or seven years. Have you thought of that possibility, sir? And do you think the American people ought to think of that possibility?

A. Yes. I think the American people ought to understand that there is no quick solution to the problem that we face there. I would not want to prophesy or predict whether it would be a matter of months or years or decades. I do not know that we had any accurate timetable on how long it would take to bring victory in World War I. I don't think anyone really knew that it would be two years or four years or six years to meet with success in World War II. I do think our cause is just. I do think our purposes and objectives are beyond question.

I do believe that America will stand united behind her men that are there. And I plan as long as I'm President to see that our forces are strong enough to protect our national interests and our right hand constantly protecting that interest with our military and that our diplomatic and political negotiations are constantly attempting to find some solution that would substitute words for bombs.

And as I have said so many times, if anyone questions our good faith and will ask us to meet them to try to reason this matter out, they will find us at the appointed place, the appointed time and the proper chair. . . .

Q. Mr. President, would you be willing to permit direct negotiations with the Vietcong forces in South Vietnam?

A. We have stated time and time again that we would negotiate with any Government, any time, any place. The Vietcong would have no difficulty in being represented and having their views presented if Hanoi for a moment decides that she wants to cease aggression, and I would not think that would be an insurmountable problem at all. I think that could be worked out. . . .

Prophecies About the War

*[The following is a necessarily incomplete catalogue
of prophecies which have been made about the Vietnamese war by those who have carried on the struggle
against the communists over the past forty years. It is
not intended to slight the able men who made the best
judgments they could in a unique, confused, and difficult situation. It should give some perspective on present statements and illuminate the need for great caution in taking great risks on the basis of necessarily
uncertain estimates.]*

FROM A SPEECH OF SENATOR JOHN F. KENNEDY
DELIVERED IN THE SENATE ON *April 6, 1954*

. . . Permit me to review briefly some of the statements concerning the progress of the war in that area,
and it will be understood why I say that either we
have not frankly and fully faced the seriousness of
the military situation, or our intelligence estimates
and those of the French have been woefully defective.

In February of 1951, for example, the late Brig. Gen.
Francis G. Brink, then head of the United States Military Advisory Group, in Indochina, told us of the
favorable turn of events in that area as a result of new

tactics designed by Gen. Jean de Lattre de Tassigny. In the fall of that same year, General de Lattre himself voiced optimism in his speech before the National Press Club here in Washington; and predicted victory, under certain conditions, in eighteen months to two years, during his visit to France.

In June of 1952, American and French officials issued a joint communiqué in Washington expressing the two countries' joint determination to bring the battle to a successful end; and Secretary of State Acheson stated at his press conference that—

"The military situation appears to be developing favorably. . . . Aggression has been checked and recent indications warrant the view that the tide is now moving in our favor. . . . We can anticipate continued favorable developments."

In March 1953, the French officials again came to Washington, again issued statements predicting victory in Indochina, and again joined with the United States in a communiqué planning military action and United States support which would achieve their new goal of decisive military victory in two years.

In May of 1953, President Eisenhower and Secretary of State Dulles told the Congress that our mutual-security program for France and Indochina would help "reduce this Communist pressure to manageable proportions." In June an American military mission headed by General O'Daniel was sent to discuss with General Navarre in Indochina the manner in which United States aid "may best contribute to the advancement of the objective of defeating the Communist forces there"; and in the fall of last year General O'Daniel stated that he was "confident that the French-trained Vietnam Army when fully organized would prevail over the rebels."

In September of 1953, French and American officials again conferred, and, in announcing a new program of extensive American aid, again issued a joint communiqué restating the objective of "an early and victorious conclusion."

On December 2, 1953, Assistant Secretary of State for Far Eastern Affairs Walter S. Robertson told the Women's National Republican Club in New York—in words almost identical with those of Secretary of State Acheson eighteen months earlier—that "in Indochina . . . we believe the tide now is turning." Later the same month Secretary of State Dulles stated that military setbacks in the area had been exaggerated; and that he did not "believe that anything that has happened upsets appreciably the timetable of General Navarre's plan," which anticipated decisive military results by about March 1955.

In February of this year, Defense Secretary Wilson said that a French victory was "both possible and probable" and that the war was going "fully as well as we expected it to at this stage. I see no reason to think Indochina would be another Korea." Also in February of this year, Under Secretary of State Smith stated that:

"The military situation in Indochina is favorable. . . . Contrary to some reports, the recent advances made by the Viet Minh are largely "real estate" operations. . . . Tactically, the French position is solid and the officers in the field seem confident of their ability to deal with the situation."

Less than two weeks ago, Admiral Radford, Chairman of the Joint Chiefs of Staff, stated that "the French are going to win." And finally, in a press conference some days prior to his speech to the Overseas Press Club in New York, Secretary of State Dulles stated that he did not "expect that there is going to be a Communist victory in Indochina"; that "in terms of Communist domination of Indochina, I do not accept that as a probability"; that "we have seen no reason to abandon the so-called Navarre plan," which meant decisive results only one year hence; and that the United States would provide whatever additional equipment was needed for victory over the Viet Minh; with the upper hand probably to be gained "by the end of the next fighting season. . . ."

STATEMENTS OF POLITICAL AND MILITARY LEADERS
ADMIRAL HARRY D. FELT *January 11, 1963*.

Admiral Harry D. Felt, commander of the United States forces in the Pacific, declared today that Communist guerrillas in South Vietnam faced "inevitable" defeat but acknowledged that difficulties existed between South Vietnamese commanders and United States military advisors.

Before leaving for Bangkok, Thailand, after a two-day visit for intensive talks with American and Vietnamese leaders here, Admiral Felt said: "I am confident the Vietnamese are going to win their war."

[In reference to the charges by U.S. officers that South

Triumph or Tragedy

Vietnamese commanders had rejected American advice and lacked aggressiveness in their fight against the Vietcong guerrillas, Felt said] "The general rule is we understand each other it is only the exception when we become a little angry with each other."
>   —*The New York Times* (Western Edition),
>   January 12, 1963 (2:1)

May 7, 1963.

A Pentagon spokesman said today that "the corner definitely has been turned" toward victory in South Vietnam and Defense Department officials are hopeful that the 12,000-man United States force there can be reduced in one to three years.

Assistant Secretary of Defense Arthur Sylvester gave this appraisal a few hours after his return with the Secretary of Defense, Robert S. McNamara, from a conference in Honolulu with high United States military and civilian officials stationed in South Vietnam.
>   —*The New York Times*, May 8, 1963 (10:2)

GENERAL HARKINS IN SAIGON.

"The Viet Cong are losing because we are steadily decreasing their areas of maneuver and the terrain over which they can move at will."

"The fortified villages are cutting the Viet Cong lifeline to the little people whom they used to 'tax' to get their piastres and their rice. It is harder for them to get into the fortified areas to kidnap youngsters and

132

turn them into recruits. Slowly, I grant you, but surely, the Viet Cong will find that there is no place to hide."
—*The New York Herald Tribune*, August 28, 1963 (1)

PRESIDENT JOHN F. KENNEDY IN TELEVISED
INTERVIEW WITH WALTER CRONKITE
September 2, 1963.

"We are prepared to continue to assist them, but I don't think that the war can be won unless the people support the effort and, in my opinion, in the last two months, the Government has gotten out of touch with the people."

"In the final analysis, it's their war. They're the ones who have to win it or lose it. We can help them, give them equipment, we can send our men out there as advisers, but they have to win it, the people of Vietnam, against the Communists."

The President said that repressions against the Buddhists "were very unwise."
—*The New York Times*, September 3, 1963 (1:8)

SECRETARY OF DEFENSE ROBERT S. MC NAMARA
AT A PRESS CONFERENCE *November 14, 1963.*

". . . We are going to bring back several hundred before the end of the year, but . . . on the question of the exact number I thought we would wait until the meeting of November 20 [the Honolulu policy conference]."
—*The New York Times*, November 15, 1963 (13:1)

November 24, 1963.

As a result of the meeting [Honolulu], White House informants said, President Johnson laid down a general policy line emphasizing the following:

First, the central point of United States policy on South Vietnam remains; namely, to assist the new government there in winning the war against the Communist Viet Cong insurgents. The adoption of all measures should be determined by their potential contribution to this overriding objective.

Second, the White House statement of October 2 on the withdrawal of American troops from South Vietnam remains in force. This statement, reflecting a decision of the National Security Council, said the program for training of Vietnamese troops should have progressed by the end of this year to the point "where one thousand United States military personnel" can be withdrawn.

—*The New York Times,* November 25, 1963 (1:4)

SECRETARY MC NAMARA BEFORE THE HOUSE
ARMED SERVICES COMMITTEE
February 18, 1964.

". . . We continue to be hopeful that we will be able to complete the training responsibilities of many of the other United States personnel now in Vietnam and gradually withdraw them over the period between now, and the end of 1965."

"I simply believe that the war in South Vietnam will be won primarily through Vietnamese effort; it is a Vietnamese war. It is a war of counter-guerrillas against guerrillas. We are only assisting them through training and logistical support."

"I think it is reasonable to expect that after four years of such training, we should be able gradually to withdraw certain of our training personnel."

[In response to questioning about the seemingly paradoxical statement on pulling troops out when the war was getting hotter, McNamara said]: "I don't believe that we as a nation should assume the primary responsibility for the war in South Vietnam."

—*The New York Times*, February 19, 1964 (8:4)

SECRETARY MC NAMARA BEFORE THE HOUSE APPROPRIATIONS COMMITTEE *March 24, 1964.*

". . . We believe that the U.S. policy in reducing U.S. military personnel in South Vietnam as the Vietnamese become capable of carrying on the logistical training and other programs which we are presently supplying to them is sound and should be continued."

SECRETARY MC NAMARA BEFORE THE ADVERTISING COUNCIL *May 6, 1964.*

". . . I think we'll begin to see signs of that progress in the months ahead. It's going to be slow, however; the war's going to be long; it can't be won quickly—no guerrilla war ever has been won quickly; this one must be won by the Vietnamese themselves. If they're to win it they just have to have a stable political structure within which to operate. We can provide advice; we can provide logistical support; we can provide training assistance, but we cannot fight the war itself. . . ."

Triumph or Tragedy

SECRETARY MC NAMARA AT A PENTAGON PRESS
CONFERENCE *April 26, 1965.*

QUESTION: In what way were the Viet Cong, which
are operating in South Vietnam, protected by the air
strikes against North Vietnam?

MC NAMARA: In two respects. First, as I say, we have
slowed down the movement of men and matériel and
this has adversely affected the Viet Cong, although I
don't wish to overemphasize the degree to which it
has affected them so far.

Secondly, the air strikes against North Vietnam and
also the increased tempo of air strikes by the Vietnamese Air Force and the U.S. Air Force in South
Vietnam have significantly and adversely affected the
morale of Viet Cong captured within the last four to
eight weeks.

The Honolulu Declaration

[The following is the text of a joint statement issued by the governments of the United States and South Vietnam on February 8, 1966, at the conclusion of the Honolulu Conference between President Lyndon B. Johnson and Premier Nguyen Cao Ky.]

Part I

The Republic of Vietnam and the United States of America jointly declare: their determination in defense against aggression, their dedication to the hopes of all the people of South Vietnam and their commitments to the search for just and stable peace.

In pursuit of these objectives the leaders of their Governments have agreed upon this declaration, which sets forth:

The purposes of the Government of Vietnam,

The purposes of the Government of the United States,

And the common commitment of both Governments.

Part II. The Purposes of the Government of Vietnam

Here in the mid-Pacific, halfway between Asia and North America, we take the opportunity to state again the aims of our Government. We are a Government—indeed a generation—of revolutionary transformation. Our people are caught up in a mortal struggle. This struggle has four sides.

[1]

We must defeat the Vietcong and those illegally fighting with them on our soil. We are the victims of an aggression directed and supported from Hanoi. That aggression—that so-called "war of national liberation" —is part of the Communist plan for the conquest of all of Southeast Asia. The defeat of that aggression is vital for the future of our people of South Vietnam.

[2]

We are dedicated to the eradication of social injustice among our people. We must bring about a true social revolution and construct a modern society in which every man can know that he has a future; that he has respect and dignity; that he has the opportunity for himself and for his children to live in an environment where all is not disappointment, despair and dejection; that the opportunities exist for the full expression of his talents and his hopes.

[3]

We must establish and maintain a stable, viable economy and build a better material life for our people.

In spite of the war, which creates many unusual and unpredictable economic situations, we are determined to continue with a policy of austerity; to make the best possible use of the assistance granted us from abroad; and to help our people achieve regular economic growth and improved material welfare.

[4]

We must build true democracy for our land and for our people. In this effort we shall continue to imbue the people with a sense of national unity, a stronger commitment to civic responsibility. We shall encourage a widened and more active participation in and contribution to the building of a free, independent, strong and peaceful Vietnam. In particular, we pledge again:

¶To formulate a democratic constitution in the months ahead, including an electoral law.

¶To take that constitution to our people for discussion and modification.

¶To seek its ratification by secret ballot.

¶To create, on the basis of elections rooted in that constitution, an elected government.

These things shall be accomplished mainly with the blood, intelligence and dedication of the Vietnamese people themselves. But in this interdependent world we shall need the help of others:

To win the war of independence; to build while we fight; to reconstruct and develop our nation when terror ceases.

To those future citizens of a free, democratic South Vietnam now fighting with the Vietcong, we take this occasion to say come and join in this national revolutionary adventure:

([Come safely to join us through the open-arms program.

([Stop killing your brothers, sisters, their elders and their children.

([Come and work through constitutional democracy to build together that life of dignity, freedom and peace those in the North would deny the people of Vietnam.

Thus, we are fighting this war. It is a military war, a war for the hearts of our people. We cannot win one without winning the other. But the war for the hearts of the people is more than a military tactic. It is a moral principle. For this we shall strive as we fight to bring about a true social revolution.

Part III. The Purposes of the Government of the United States

[1]

The United States of America is joined with the people and Government of Vietnam to prevent aggression. This is the purpose of the determined effort of the American armed forces now engaged in Vietnam. The United States seeks no bases. It seeks no colonial presence. It seeks to impose no alliance or alignment. It seeks only to prevent aggression, and its pledge to that purpose is firm. It aims simply to help a people and government who are determined to help themselves.

[2]

The United States is pledged to the principles of the self-determination of peoples, and of government by the consent of the governed. It therefore gives its full support to the purpose of free elections proclaimed by the Government of South Vietnam and to the principle of open arms and amnesty for all who turn from terror toward peace and rural construction. The United States will give its full support to measures of social revolution, including land reform based upon the principle of building upward from the hopes and purposes of all the people of Vietnam.

[3]

Just as the United States is pledged to play its part in the worldwide attack upon hunger, ignorance and disease, so in Vietnam it will give special support to the work of the people of that country to build even while they fight.

We have helped and we will help them—to stabilize the economy, to increase the production of food, to spread the light of education, to stamp out disease.

[4]

The purpose of the United States remains a purpose of peace. The United States Government and the Government of Vietnam will continue in the future, as they have in the past, to press the quest for a peaceful settlement in every forum. The world knows the harsh and negative response these efforts have thus far received. The world should know, too, that the United

States Government and the Government of Vietnam remain determined that no path to peace shall be unexplored. Within the framework of their international commitments, the United States and Vietnam aim to create with others a stable peace in Southeast Asia which will permit the governments and peoples of the region to devote themselves to lifting the condition of man. With the understanding and support of the Government of Vietnam, the peace offensive of the United States Government and the Government of South Vietnam will continue until peace is secured.

Part IV. The Common Commitment

The President of the United States and the chief of state and Prime Minister of the Republic of Vietnam are thus pledged again:

To defense against aggression,
To the work of social revolution,
To the goal of free self-government,
To the attack on hunger, ignorance and disease,
And to the unending quest for peace.

—Honolulu, February 8, 1966

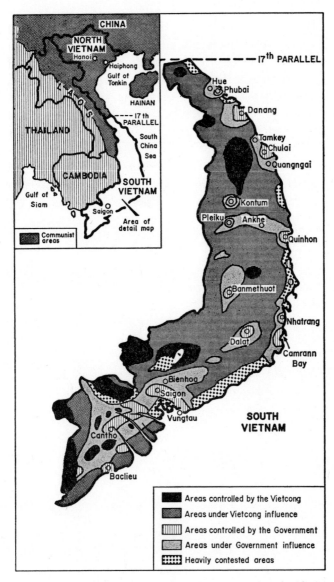

This map shows the relative territorial positions of each side in Vietnam as of early 1966.

About the Author

RICHARD N. GOODWIN holds bachelor's degrees from Tufts University and Harvard Law School. Admitted to the Massachusetts Bar in 1958, he served as a law clerk to Supreme Court Justice Felix Frankfurter, and in 1960 as Assistant to the then Senator John F. Kennedy. In 1961 Mr. Goodwin became Assistant Special Counsel to President Kennedy. Subsequently he served as Deputy Assistant Secretary of State for inter-American affairs, Secretary-General of the International Peace Corps secretariat, and as Special Assistant to President Johnson. At present Mr. Goodwin is a Fellow of The Center for Advanced Studies at Wesleyan University. He and his wife make their home in Middletown, Connecticut.